IGNORANT
ARMIES

BY GWYNNE DYER

War (1985)
The Defence of Canada (1990)

IGNORANT ARMIES

SLIDING INTO WAR IN IRAQ

GWYNNE DYER

National Library of Canada Cataloguing in Publication Data

Dyer, Gwynne
    Ignorant armies : sliding into war in Iraq / Gwynne Dyer.

ISBN 0-7710-2977-2

1. United States – Foreign relations – 2001- .   2. United States – Military relations – Iraq.   3. Iraq – Military relations – United States. 4. United States – Foreign relations – Middle East.   5. Middle East – Foreign relations – United States.   I. Title.

DS79.755.D95 2003   327.73056'09'0511   C2003-900955-6

We acknowledge the financial support of the Government of Canada through the Book Publishing Industry Development Program and that of the Government of Ontario through the Ontario Media Development Corporation's Ontario Book Initiative. We further acknowledge the support of the Canada Council for the Arts and the Ontario Arts Council for our publishing program.

Typeset in Minion by M&S, Toronto
Printed and bound in Canada

McClelland & Stewart Ltd.
The Canadian Publishers
481 University Avenue
Toronto, Ontario
M5G 2E9
www.mcclelland.com

1 2 3 4 5   07 06 05 04 03

This book is for Kate, who wasn't around yet when other books got dedicated to her older brothers and sister.

And we are here as on a darkling plain
Swept with confused alarms of struggle and flight,
Where ignorant armies clash by night.

— from "Dover Beach" by Matthew Arnold

CONTENTS

INTRODUCTION

If historical ingratitude were a crime, the chattering classes of the West would be facing life sentences at hard labour. The luckiest generation in history, the people who got their future back because the Third World War was cancelled, think that the world has changed forever just because a few terrorists have chosen them as targets.

About three thousand human beings were killed in the terrorist attacks on New York and Washington on September 11, 2001. That makes "9/11" the worst single terrorist incident in history, and it all played out on live television, so the immediate shock and outrage were entirely understandable. But the actual loss of life on that day was on the same order as the monthly death toll from traffic accidents in the United States – and there was almost no follow-up to those terrorist attacks, whereas the other loss occurs every month.

Numbers do matter. At least half the American population would have died in a Third World War fought with nuclear weapons. Therefore the Third World War was an awesome possibility, one that could actually have ended American history. Only one American in a hundred thousand died on September 11, and not one in a million has been killed in terrorist attacks since then, so the new terrorism, viewed in this context, is virtually a non-event.

It is the media coverage that gives terrorism such huge apparent importance, of course – modern terrorism is almost entirely a media phenomenon – but it is nevertheless astonishing how big it has made this event seem, and how long it has kept it inflated. Even in 2003, the terrorist attacks on the United States in 2001 still shape American and Western foreign policy – or at least they are still being used, without much dissent, as justification for policies that may in fact have other motives and goals. September 11 did not change the world, but it is being used in an attempt to change the world.

This is not 1939, when great moral and ideological issues were involved, or even 1914, when at least great armies were involved. For all its modern technological trappings, this feels more like one of the colonial wars of the late nineteenth century – say, the Spanish-American War of 1898, Washington's first excursion into imperialism. The pretext for the American attack on the Spanish empire on that occasion was an explosion that sank the battleship *Maine* in Havana harbour, killing over a thousand Americans. There was actually no evidence to connect the Spanish government with the disaster (sound familiar?), but the war was popular with the American public because it was over quickly, cost little, and allowed the United States to control Cuba for quite a few years, the Philippines for half a century, and Puerto Rico and American Samoa for good.

But the Spanish-American War was really a sideshow. The main event at the turn of the last century was the Anglo-Boer

War of 1899–1902, when Britain, the world's greatest power, cooked up an unjustified war of aggression against the little Afrikaner republics of southern Africa, not because they were nasty – though they were, at least towards foreigners and blacks – but because they had one valuable resource that the imperial power craved: gold. Then, as now, almost everybody else disapproved of the war, but chose not to lie down in front of the steamroller. Then – and maybe now – the war turned out to be a lot longer and harder than the planners calculated. And though Britain won it in the end, the war marked the beginning of a steep half-century decline that ended its superpower status. Could that happen to America too?

Almost certainly not: the United States today is far more dominant, relative to the other great powers, than Britain was in 1899. But there could be a modest silver lining if things get bad in Iraq, in the sense that if the Bush administration has a thoroughly miserable experience in the Middle East over the next year or so, the American right wing might be cured of its current fantasy that the United States can actually run the world. We should not wish for the lesson to be taught in this way, however, for the price would be too high, and sooner or later the unilateralist tide in the United States is bound to recede with or without disasters in the Middle East.

How bad could it get? The worst-case scenario is a bloody ground war in Iraq, followed by a lengthy and debilitating American occupation; the overthrow of existing, pro-Western regimes in Jordan, Saudi Arabia, Egypt, or Pakistan by Islamist revolutionaries; the expulsion of the Palestinians from their remaining footholds west of the Jordan River (which would foreclose any hope of general Arab-Israeli peace for the indefinite future); a large rise in oil prices and a prolonged global recession; and more and bigger terrorist attacks by Islamist groups on Western targets than has been the norm up to now. That is a lengthy tale of woe, but not all of it is likely to happen. Even if it did, it wouldn't be the end of the world, or even of the Middle East. There have been bigger upheavals in the past half-century, and most of us are still here.

Nevertheless, the terrorist attacks on the United States on September 11, 2001, set in motion an avalanche of events, clearly connected in some senses though hugely different in character and motive. The largest of those events, it now appears, will be a war of considerable size in the Middle East, and it is worth the effort to try to understand the goals and strategies of the major players, American, Islamist, Israeli, and Iraqi. What did the planners of al-Qaeda actually hope to achieve with their attacks on the United States, and how serious a threat to the status quo are they? How has American strategy responded and mutated in the months since then – and in particular, why did the subject change from al-Qaeda to Iraq? Has there really been a revolution in military affairs that now enables technologically advanced military powers to fight and win wars virtually without casualties, and could it be the foundation of a lasting *Pax Americana*? Is Saddam Hussein dangerous to anybody other than his immediate neighbours? Indeed, is he even dangerous to them any more?

I should mention that I do not oppose war in the right cause on principle. I supported using military force under United Nations authority to drive Saddam Hussein's army out of occupied Kuwait in the Gulf War of 1990–91 because invading your neighbours is wrong. More recently I supported military action in Bosnia and later in Kosovo, because attempted genocide is also wrong. My unease about the motives and probable consequences of the Second Gulf War (as it will probably be called) are specific to this occasion.

To write a book about a war before it starts – without even being certain that it will start – is to give too many hostages to fortune. But it still seems worthwhile to try to make sense of the recent past and present, especially as the near future may not make much sense at all.

CHAPTER I

A NEEDLESS WAR

"... the interests of Muslims and socialists converge in the fight against the Crusaders. . . . It is going to be a great battle, and we are going to defeat the enemy. The fighting should be in the name of God only, not in the name of national ideologies, nor to seek victory for the ignorant governments that rule all Arab states, including Iraq."

– Osama bin Laden, tape broadcast
on al-Jazeera, February 12, 2003

"What George W. Bush is proposing, taking military action against Iraq to eliminate Saddam Hussein, will effectively mean that Osama bin Laden will have won. . . . There is a good chance that a domino effect will come into play. We could see Saudi Arabia fall, Kuwait fall, Jordan fall, Egypt fall and the entire region being swept up in a sea of anti-Western, Islamic fundamentalism. . . . The invasion of Iraq is the quickest path to losing the war on terror and giving legitimacy to the criminal who attacked the U.S. . . . on September 11."

– Former UN arms inspector and
ex-U.S. Marine officer Scott Ritter, London, July 2002

"You should never trust the experts," wrote Lord Salisbury in 1877, two decades before he wound up as Britain's prime minister during the Anglo-Boer War. "If you believe the doctors, nothing is wholesome; if you believe the theologians, nothing is innocent; if you believe the soldiers, nothing is safe." In other words: Never ask the barber if you need a haircut, or the military about the need for war.

But something strange started happening recently, because it wasn't the soldiers who were agitating for an attack on Iraq: not in the Pentagon, and not among America's allies either. Salisbury's warning applies with full force to the "terrorism experts," but the military professionals who have to fight wars on the ground (air forces are a different matter) have been remarkably unenthusiastic about the whole enterprise. Military discipline and constitutional propriety prevent senior American army officers from openly expressing their misgivings about the policies of their political superiors, but it was striking how, in the course of 2002, successive U.S. army war plans for invading Iraq, drawn up at the behest of the White House, were routinely leaked to the press almost immediately –

as though the generals hoped that public ridicule of their plans would save them from having to carry them out.

As 2002 drew to an end, ordinary Americans (and to a lesser extent other people in the West too) still saw the threat of further terrorist outrages on the scale of the World Trade Center and Pentagon attacks as a real possibility, and wanted action on that front. Their willingness to support a war against Iraq as well, however, depended mainly on whether they bought the Bush administration's carefully choreographed insinuations (never accompanied by evidence) about a link between Saddam Hussein and the terrorists of al-Qaeda.

The post–September 11 chill kept the mainstream American media from questioning the administration's motives and strategy too closely, the military kept their heads down and their mouths shut, and Congress essentially gave President George W. Bush a blank cheque, but from the beginning it proved very hard for the White House to make a coherent case for an attack on Iraq. The difficulties got considerably worse in September-October 2002, when North Korea, the only non-Muslim member of the "axis of evil," revealed that it still had a secret nuclear weapons program running despite its 1994 agreement to stop it. U.S. Defense Secretary Donald Rumsfeld tried to keep the timetable for an American attack on Iraq on track by assuring the public at a December 23 Pentagon briefing that "we are capable of fighting two major regional conflicts. We're capable of winning decisively in one and swiftly defeating in the case of the other. And let there be no doubt about it." Other countries might quail at the prospect of a two-front war, but in Rumsfeld's view the United States is so powerful that it's not even a problem.

This was not exactly the reassurance the American public was looking for, however, especially as somewhere in the back of their collective memory there is a dim recollection that the Korean War had not been quite as quick and cheap as the Gulf War. By early January 2003, President Bush was intervening personally to calm American fears. Recalling his 2002 trip to South Korea, he told the press, "The United States has no intention of invading North Korea. I said that right there in South Korea. In Kim Jong Il's neighborhood, I spoke clearly. I said 'we won't invade you.'" Not North Korea. Just Iraq.

On the one hand we had Iraq, a nation that denied it had any existing nuclear, chemical, biological, or radiological weapons programs (though it certainly had them all before the Gulf War of 1990–91). It had allowed in United Nations arms inspectors, who were crawling all over the country in search of the programs for developing "weapons of mass destruction" that the U.S. government insisted had been restarted by Saddam Hussein. Up to the end of January they had found nothing apart from fifteen empty warheads for short-range 122-mm rockets that had originally been designed to be filled with poison gas. Yet the Bush administration was straining at the leash to launch an invasion of Iraq whose purpose, according to the rhetoric in daily use until September 2002, was "regime change": in practice, nothing less than the killing of Saddam and his sons, and the restructuring of Iraqi society under American leadership.

On the other hand there was the fanatical hermit kingdom of North Korea, the world's last Stalinist state, which has been America's avowed enemy for more than fifty years. North Korea had an active nuclear weapons program (and enough plutonium to make a couple of warheads, according to Rumsfeld), it had just kicked UN arms inspectors out, and it had announced its intention to withdraw from the Nuclear Non-Proliferation Treaty. Moreover, it had already demonstrated that it had missiles capable of reaching farther than Japan, with longer-range ones capable of reaching the United States allegedly under development, and it was notorious for selling its advanced weapons technology to all sorts of places where Washington would prefer it not to go. Yet the Bush administration promised under no circumstances whatever to try to disarm this adversary by military means.

And what had this all to do with Bush's war on terror anyway? That "war" was a response to al-Qaeda's terrorist attacks of September 2001, and there is absolutely no evidence that any of the alleged members of the "axis of evil" (Iraq, Iran, and North Korea) had anything to do with those attacks. Indeed, it is almost unimaginable that the rulers of any of those countries would have any dealings with the planners of the September attacks. Al-Qaeda's leaders are Sunni Muslim religious extremists for whom Communists, Shia Muslims, and worst of all secular Arabs who share their own Sunni Muslim heritage are the enemies of God. North Korea's leader, Kim Jong Il, is a Communist; Iran's leaders, whatever their internal disputes, are all Shia Muslims; and Iraq's dictator,

Saddam Hussein, is a secular socialist of Marxist background who may not privately be a believing Muslim at all.

In other words, the story does not make sense. Bad things have happened already, and others will probably follow, but the explanations for how it all joins up that are being offered to the peoples of the West by the leaders of the United States and some of its allies simply do not hold water.

Each international crisis has some new features that make it feel unique to the people living through it, but the sequence of events that began at the World Trade Center and the Pentagon and may end in the ruins of Baghdad or in some other, yet unknown location is not really about religion or terrorism. It's the same old business of power and interests and force, dressed up in new garb – and that applies as much to al-Qaeda as to the United States of America.

For the United States, there are a variety of motives in play, from a simple concern for the security of its citizens to concerns about the future security of its oil supplies, and from family vendetta ("he tried to kill my dad") to a pseudo-historical argument about the right and duty of the United States to take charge of the world for its own good. Nothing new there, either in terms of American history or of the way other countries have behaved. The Islamist revolutionaries of the Arab world seem like a different beast at first glance, but whatever their religious quirks they are real-world players: their primary objective is to bring people like themselves to power in major Arab countries, as part of a longer-range program for overthrowing Western dominance in their part of the world. Twenty other movements like it, fuelled at least in part by religious extremism, have briefly flourished in one part or another of the Third World at some time in the past two centuries, from the Indian Mutiny and the Mahdi's revolt in Sudan to the Boxer Rebellion in China and the Mau Mau uprising in Kenya. Technological change has made it possible for al-Qaeda to operate on a wider international stage, but that's the extent of the difference. And Saddam Hussein's objective could not be more traditional: just to go on drawing breath.

It isn't all that big a crisis, either: no great powers will be going to war with each other. At worst, it may evolve ("skid" is perhaps the better word) into a major Middle Eastern upheaval on the order of 1967 or 1973, but even that is less than likely. And the actual fighting in Iraq, if there is any, will probably involve some tens of thousands killed on the Iraqi side and hundreds or a few thousand American military dead. It could be far less than that, but even the pessimistic estimates are very low by historical standards. The country now called Iraq has been conquered at least twenty times before in its long history, and every time the butcher's bill was much higher than it is likely to be this time. As for the United States, any one of twenty Civil War battles killed more American soldiers than are likely to die in the course of conquering Iraq. And yet it's all going to seem like a very big deal. It's all going to *be* a very big deal, because sensibilities have changed.

They have changed only quite recently. During the Second World War, the Russians didn't buckle although they were losing close to a million people a month to enemy action and starvation, and even the United States accepted the deaths of almost ten thousand American soldiers per month without flinching. By the time of the Vietnam War in the 1960s, however, a thousand American soldiers killed a month was seen as an intolerable sacrifice – and by the time some thirty thousand American soldiers were sent to help in a United Nations– backed humanitarian intervention in the anarchy of Somalia in 1993, the loss of only nineteen Americans in a botched foray into a no-go part of Mogadishu was enough to turn the American public against the whole operation. Between five hundred and a thousand Somalis were killed in the fighting, but in terms of U.S. losses, the generation of Americans who fought at Okinawa and the Battle of the Bulge would have seen it as a bad company-level firefight. In 1993, American public opinion was so shocked by the casualty toll, and in particular by a video clip of one dead American soldier being dragged through the streets of Mogadishu past a mob of cheering Somalis, that President Bill Clinton pulled the entire U.S. armed force out of Somalia shortly afterwards – and a big-budget feature film, *Black Hawk Down*, was made about the "disaster" in 2001.

The lesson of Somalia was taken to heart by the U.S. army, and from 1993 until very recently the unwritten rule at the Pentagon was that you must never cross the "Mogadishu line": no American forces should be committed to any overseas operation that is not in a vital national interest if more than twenty soldiers are likely to be killed as a result. The number was arbitrarily linked to the Mogadishu experience, and would depend in practice on how the twenty soldiers die – All on one day? Were there cameras present? – but the army's conclusion was entirely valid: the deaths of just twenty American soldiers could easily result in a collapse of public support for the operation in question, and in lasting damage to the army's ability to mount other operations overseas.

This is not a deplorable phenomenon. Soldiers' deaths used to happen offstage, far from the view of civilian society, and the only images civilians saw of the battlefield were in panoramic paintings that softened and glorified the slaughter. That traditional vision of battle as a noble enterprise died in the trenches of the First World War alongside 8 million conscripted citizen-soldiers, but even after that the old social discipline held for another generation. What finally did in that kind of war was television, which began to give civilians at home an inkling of what was actually happening to their sons, brothers, husbands in battle. As a result, the public's sensibility about war changed fundamentally – and it is changing everywhere, not just in the rich, comfortable West. The granddaughters of Russian women who numbly waited for their sons to die in the slaughterhouse battles of the Second World War now demonstrate in the streets of Moscow against the war in Chechnya. They occasionally even show up there and snatch their sons back from the military machine. You have to go to somewhere like India to hear people still using the word "glory" when they talk about war, and even there it is fading fast now that nuclear weapons have entered the equation.

There is a paradox here, of course. While the change in popular sensibilities in the West between 1940 and 1970 made battlefield deaths into a politically fraught issue that has never gone away again, the civilian megadeaths that were calmly envisioned by the prevailing strategy of nuclear deterrence did not elicit the same outrage at all. A handful of activists worked tirelessly to raise public consciousness on this issue, but after the panic of the later 1950s seemed to have found its resolution in the relatively happy outcome of the Cuban missile crisis of 1962, popular anxiety about nuclear war never again stayed high for very long. Perhaps it had to do with the fact there were no pictures on our television screens of people dying in nuclear explosions, apart from grainy old footage from Hiroshima, so nobody felt the horror of what was being planned in the same way that they could see, on television, during the Vietnam War, the reality of contemporary ground combat. At any rate, the strategic air commands of the world got a free ride while the armies got a big and permanent problem: nobody likes what they do any more.

In the bad old days, what the United States is now proposing to do in Iraq would not be a problem at all. Like the imperial powers of previous centuries, it has total strategic dominance over the region and a sufficient technological lead in weaponry to be able to inflict casualties on the local opposition at a ratio of ten, fifty, even a hundred to one. What that meant in the old days was that if you wanted to knock over the local ruler, you just went in and did it, and so long as no other great power objected, that was the end of the matter. You lost a few soldiers, but nobody back home saw them die and nobody but their families really minded. Lots of local people died, but nobody outside the country saw that either, not even their relatives in neighbouring countries. The Dutch did it in Indonesia, the French did it in North Africa, the United States did it all over Central America and the Caribbean, the British did it pretty well everywhere (including Iraq), and they all got away with it. But not any more.

Now there are journalists with the troops all the time, including lots of television crews, and even though far too many of them live off the briefings and go around dressed up in bits of military kit rather than doing their proper jobs, the story does get back – with pictures – that our young men and women are getting killed, often in very unpleasant ways. Then, if we're talking about American casualties, there's another TV crew at Dover Air Force Base in Delaware to film the body bags coming off the plane (an alternative name for the "Mogadishu line" was the "Dover criterion"), followed by local television interviews with the parents of the deceased asking them how they feel about the war now. It doesn't have to be good journalism; in fact, it often isn't. But the media do pay attention to soldiers' deaths, because people quite rightly feel responsible for having sent those young people to die in a way that they don't feel responsible for young people who die in car crashes or street violence at home – and pretty soon the public starts feeling queasy about the consequences of its government's policies. The more deaths, the more popular unease – and though the Mogadishu line may have moved a bit since

September 11, it hasn't disappeared over the horizon. In fact, most senior U.S. army officers suspect that it won't be that hard to find at all.

Meanwhile, on the other side of the line, journalists from al-Jazeera, the independent Arabic-language satellite TV channel, are everywhere in Iraq, sending shocking footage of civilian Iraqi victims of the war back to their newsroom in Qatar. From there it goes up to the satellite and straight down onto the dishes throughout the Arab world, where it is the one uncensored and trusted source of news. This is footage that most Arab governments would rather their citizens did not see, because if you aren't prepared to defy the United States, then you don't want your citizens to get upset and demand that you do. But more than 10 per cent of homes throughout the Arab world, some 35 million people, get al-Jazeera directly, and a lot of other people get the story at one remove. So what the United States does in Iraq (with the best of intentions, of course) becomes the spark that sets the dry tinder alight – and there is no part of the world with more dry tinder lying around waiting for a spark. Not one of the eighteen Arabic-speaking countries is a democracy. None, apart from a few of the tiniest oil-rich sheikdoms, delivers prosperity to all its citizens. Not one of the existing Arab regimes has the faintest idea how to come to terms with Israel, the dwarf superpower in their midst, and most of them have been in power (without doing much that was useful with that power) since time out of mind. So when you show up their helplessness and irrelevance, as an American attack on Iraq will show them up, and al-Jazeera underlines it by its impartial professional coverage of what is actually happening, some of those deeply unpopular and illegitimate regimes may topple.

Young King Abdullah II of Jordan, only three years on the throne and with a population that is 70 per cent Palestinian, could be the first to go, for Palestinians don't care that Saddam Hussein is a murderous thug who has never done them any actual good. He is the only Arab leader who openly defies the Israelis, and they love him for it. During the Gulf War of 1990–91, the Palestinians of Jordan were so intoxicated by Saddam's promise to smite Israel with his missiles (he did fire thirty-nine Scud missiles in the direction of Israel, though no Israelis died, except one who had a heart attack) that the "Plucky Little King," as Western journalists liked to call King Hussein, had to pretend to agree with them. King Hussein didn't really oppose sending a U.S.-dominated coalition of forces to drive Saddam out of occupied Kuwait, but he had to adopt that position, at least for a while, in order to placate the anger of his Palestinian subjects. The United States was very understanding about the PLK's dilemma in 1990, and it might even be understanding about King Abdullah's today, but the younger man simply doesn't have the credibility in Jordan that King Hussein had after two wars with Israel and forty-six years on the throne. Even aligning himself temporarily with Saddam, as Hussein did in 1990, might not be enough to save Abdullah.

Elsewhere in the Arab world, the two countries with the most imperilled regimes are the richest one and the biggest one. Saudi Arabia sits on an ocean of oil, but half of its 22 million people are under twenty-five years old, half the working-age population is unemployed, and per capita income is down by two-thirds since 1980 – which might have some distant relationship to the fact that fifteen of the nineteen hijackers on September 11 were Saudi Arabian citizens. Egypt is a sophisticated and metropolitan society of 65 million people that was once relatively prosperous and is now poor, where three military dictators, passing power down from one to the next without any consultation, have ruled the country without great success for the past fifty years. But if Saudi Arabia falls into the hands of anti-Western Islamists, so do the largest oil reserves in the world and the two holiest cities of Islam. If Egypt falls, so do the Suez Canal and Cairo, the cultural and entertainment capital of the Arab world – New York and Los Angeles all in one. Trying to destroy Saddam Hussein's regime might be a good idea if nobody else got hurt, but the reality could be very ugly.

Given the potential for large American casualties and far larger numbers of Iraqi deaths if Saddam Hussein manages to force the U.S. into street-fighting in Baghdad, and the likelihood that there will be a lot of broken crockery elsewhere in the region if that happens, why has the U.S. government decided that its most urgent task is to destroy Saddam Hussein's regime? That is a very good question, to which the answer, in Washington, is generally that Saddam Hussein has "weapons of mass destruction." Even the hawks in Washington do not seriously claim that Saddam had anything to do with the terrorist attacks of September 2001, and he has no way of delivering these alleged weapons on American targets himself, even if he were so minded. But he does hate the United States, they argue, so he might give them to "terrorists" (presumably belonging to al-Qaeda or its many lesser clones) who would smuggle them into the United States and kill huge numbers of Americans. Therefore the United States must "disarm" Saddam (incidentally killing him in the process) and put a different regime in his place in Iraq. So let us look into this question of the alleged weapons of mass destruction that are the justification, or at least the pretext, for a U.S. attack on Iraq. What are they, how dangerous would they be, and where is the proof that they still exist, or in some cases ever did exist?

Q: Mr. President, how can you be sure that Saddam Hussein has weapons of mass destruction?
A: We kept the receipts.

"I do not understand the squeamishness about the use of gas," wrote Winston Churchill, then president of Britain's Air Council, in 1919. "I am strongly in favour of using poisonous gas against uncivilised tribes." But that was before the use of poison gas in war was declared illegal under the 1925 Geneva Protocol banning chemical weapons, and half a century before chemical weapons were included in a new category called "weapons of mass destruction."

Weapons of mass destruction (WMD) come in three kinds: nuclear, biological, and chemical, and about all they have in common is that they are illegal for at least some countries to possess or use. They are certainly not equally destructive, and in the case of chemical weapons they are not really about mass destruction at all. Chemical weapons are battlefield weapons, basically a different kind of artillery, which is how they were used when they were first deployed on the battlefield in France in 1915. Their use was outlawed after the First World War, in which they were the cause of hundreds of thousands of deaths and lingering disabilities, some eventually leading to death, in an even larger number of ex-combatants. The fact that neither side used them in the Second World War, although enormous stocks were built up by the major participants just in case, was largely due to the fact that nobody saw any lasting military advantage in using them. Indeed, the protocol was not violated at all (apart from the suspected small-scale use of chemical weapons by the Egyptian and Soviet forces that intervened in the Yemeni civil war in the 1960s) until Iraq's war with Iran in 1980–88. But then, poison gas is not a useful battlefield weapon except in First World War–style circumstances, where large numbers of infantry soldiers face each other in densely populated lines of trenches.

That was why Saddam Hussein used it. Once Iraq's initial offensives into Iran had failed and his badly outnumbered troops were pushed back into their own territory, the desperate Iraqi army began using mustard gas (which produces blisters on the skin and inside the lungs) to break up the Iranian mass attacks. By 1983–84 the Iraqis were also using tabun, a nerve gas, in a limited way, and by the end of the war they had developed and begun using sarin, a more lethal nerve gas.

They also used cyanide gas, which kills instantaneously. They did this with the full knowledge and implicit consent of the United States, which had become a de facto ally of Iraq in order to prevent a victory for Ayatollah Khomeini's fundamentalist and anti-American regime in Iran.

Declassified U.S. government documents published in the *Washington Post* in December 2002 revealed that Secretary of State George Schultz was given intelligence reports in November 1983 reporting the "almost daily use of CW" (chemical weapons) by Saddam Hussein's military. Less than a month later, President Ronald Reagan signed a secret order instructing his administration to do "whatever was necessary and legal" to prevent Saddam Hussein from losing the war, and in December 1983 Donald Rumsfeld (now President George W. Bush's defence secretary) travelled to Baghdad to tell Saddam personally that the U.S. government was willing to help and wished to restore full diplomatic relations. Rumsfeld has subsequently claimed that he did "caution" Saddam against using illegal weapons, but there is no mention of such a warning in State Department notes of the meeting. Certainly no action was taken, and in the following years the American government allowed vital ingredients for chemical weapons to be exported to Iraq, together with dozens of biological agents, including various strains of anthrax.

From 1983 onwards, Iraq was regularly supplied with intelligence on Iranian troop movements and dispositions gathered by the American-operated AWACS aircraft (Airborne Warning and Control System) in the Gulf, and starting in 1986

U.S. air force officers on detached duty secretly helped their Iraqi counterparts to interpret American-supplied AWACS and satellite imagery to plan attacks against Iran – including offensives in the Fao peninsula during which there was lavish use of poison gas. The White House wielded its influence to kill a Senate bill that sought to punish Saddam Hussein for resorting to poison gas by banning the export of American military equipment and advanced technology to Iraq. The U.S. government even helped Baghdad to cover up when the Iraqi air force attacked the town of Halabja in northern Iraq with nerve gas in 1988, believing it to be still occupied by Iranian troops. In fact, the Iranians had withdrawn the previous day, and the gas instead killed sixty-eight hundred innocent Kurdish civilians who had just returned to their homes. (This is the incident now exploited rhetorically by President Bush in his frequent assertions that Saddam Hussein "gassed his own people." At the time the Pentagon came up with the idea of defending Saddam by partly blaming Iran for the atrocity, and U.S. diplomats were instructed to push that lie.)

As many as a hundred thousand of Iran's half-million war deaths in 1980–88 were due to Iraq's use of poison gas (which the Iranians eventually reciprocated), but delivering it on a battlefield is a heavy industrial operation as complex and demanding as an artillery barrage. And just as in a conventional artillery barrage, the normal "kill ratio" for a poison gas bombardment would rarely exceed one or two enemy soldiers per shell. To kill those hundred thousand Iranians, Iraq probably used around a hundred thousand poison gas shells and bombs. Gas is a nasty battlefield weapon, in other words, but hardly a weapon of mass destruction that would hold much appeal for terrorists. You would probably cause far more carnage, and have a far higher level of confidence that your weapon would work, if you used a nail bomb in a terrorist attack instead of a poison gas canister of the same size and weight. That was the lesson the Japanese cult Aum Shinrikyo learned in 1995 when it released nerve gas, which it had produced in its own lab, in the Tokyo subway system, and only managed to kill twelve people.

Fifteen years after the Iran-Iraq War, does Saddam Hussein's regime still have poison gas weapons? Maybe, although the UN arms inspectors who spent almost eight years in Iraq after the Gulf War certainly found and destroyed the vast majority of Iraq's stocks. President Bush's allegation in his January 2003 State of the Union speech that Iraq has failed to account for "25,000 litres of anthrax, 38,000 litres of botulism toxin, 500 tons of sarin, mustard gas and VX nerve agent and thousands of [short-range warheads] capable of delivering chemical weapons" is based solely on mathematical calculations using questionable data and is probably a vast exaggeration. Still, nobody would be astonished if Saddam did still have a few bits and pieces tucked away somewhere. Would he ever use such weapons against American forces, if he does still have them? No, except perhaps in a last-ditch battle for Baghdad, for it would in effect be a revenge from the grave. The United States has reserved the right to reply to an Iraqi use of chemical or biological weapons with nuclear weapons: only if Saddam knew that he was already a "dead man walking" might he give such an order. The same applies in spades to any use of chemical or biological weapons against Israel, in the event that he still has missiles capable of delivering such an attack.

But skip past the present, probably terminal crisis faced by Saddam and imagine he is still there three or five years from now. Would he give poison gas or biological weapons to terrorists, as the Bush administration professes to fear? There is no evidence that he has done so in the past, and his history of sponsoring terrorism in general is considerably less worrisome than that of some other Middle Eastern regimes, notably those of Iran, Syria, and Libya, that may well possess such weapons. In particular, Saddam would be extremely unlikely to have anything to do with Islamist terrorists like the members of al-Qaeda, whose main objective is to overthrow secular Arab regimes like his. If terrorists really want to gas people, they'd find it simpler to make the poison gas themselves on location – it's not that hard, and you avoid the border-crossing problem – or to steal it from the stocks that all the great powers still maintain for "training purposes." (In western Siberia the Russians still have a vast arsenal of warheads loaded with nerve agents, much of it stored in warehouses secured with bicycle padlocks.) They'd do even better if they simply chose a different weapon.

Well, then, how about biological weapons? Surely they are genuinely weapons of mass destruction. The answer is that nobody really knows how dangerous they are, for they have never been used in war, apart from Japanese attacks on eleven

Chinese cities before and during the Second World War, and there are no reliable medical data on the effects of those attacks. Aum Shinrikyo tried releasing both botulism toxin and anthrax in Tokyo (prepared once again in its own lab, with no help from "rogue states"), but moved on to nerve gas because the biological agents had no discernible effect at all. The only other example we have of actual use of bio-weapons is the post–September 11 anthrax attacks in the United States, when a still unidentified terrorist – probably a native-born American loner who stole a weaponized strain of anthrax from a U.S. government lab – spread both disease and panic through the mail. Millions of terrified people went through the ritual of running out of buildings and waiting around outside for hours in response to hoaxes, but the actual loss of life was four or five people: the equivalent of one bad car crash.

In order to pose the sort of threat that would qualify it as a genuine weapon of mass destruction, a biological weapon must have the ability to be dispersed secretly and effectively in a way that will quickly kill many thousands of human beings. In developed countries, this is harder than it seems, since the usual human immunities mean that most diseases spread relatively slowly, and normal medical reporting procedures ensure that outbreaks will quickly be detected and contained by vaccination and quarantine measures. The one disease that causes a lot of worry is smallpox, against which most people have no immunity as vaccinations ceased once it was eradicated in the wild over thirty years ago. So far as is known, the only surviving samples of the virus are in closely guarded government laboratories in the United States and Russia, but it is possible that various secret biological warfare establishments have retained their own supplies "just in case." Doubts have been expressed about all the major powers in this regard from time to time, but what about the members of President Bush's "axis of evil"? Could they have the smallpox virus hidden away somewhere?

North Korea certainly could, as it has been under the same paranoid, ruthless, and highly secretive regime since the late 1940s, long enough ago that its agents could easily have acquired the smallpox virus in the wild. It is marginally possible that Iran might have the virus too: smallpox was no longer freely available when the current regime took over in 1978, but it might have been inherited from the Shah's ambitious military program, which had been working hard to expand Iran's power for twenty years before that. Least likely is Iraq, where the Ba'ath Party did not arrive in power (apart from one brief nine-month stint) until 1968. By the time the Ba'athist regime got itself organized, it would have been quite hard for it to lay its hands on smallpox virus, and the previous Iraqi regimes were most unlikely to have been working on biological weapons.

Even if one or more of these countries does have the smallpox virus, and could come up with a plausible motive for releasing it or giving it to terrorists to use (a difficult thing to imagine, for what advantage could they gain from it?), how much damage would it actually do? The most realistic measure of the level of threat, perhaps, is the fact that the entire population of Western countries could be protected from smallpox infection by a program of vaccination, but the vaccine kills about one in a million of the people who take it – and that is regarded as an unacceptable cost.

If you want to know the real view of military experts about the value of the various unconventional weapons that normally are grouped together as weapons of mass destruction, just follow the money. Of the hundreds of billions of dollars that have been spent on WMD in the past sixty years, at least 98 per cent has gone to nuclear weapons. Chemical and biological weapons are interesting curiosities on which you spend just enough to ensure that you are not surprised by some unexpected advance; nuclear weapons are the Real Thing, and for a long time the great powers behaved as if you could not have enough. Since 1945, the United States and Russia have built fifty to sixty thousand nuclear weapons (although at least half of them have subsequently been recycled). Five other countries – Britain, France, Israel, China, and India, in order of when they went nuclear – own between a hundred and a thousand nuclear warheads each, and Pakistan, the newest nuclear-weapons power, has between twenty and sixty.

There has long been anxiety that one or more of these true weapons of mass destruction might fall into the hands of terrorists. Hundreds of scholarly articles, media stories, and secret government reports have speculated about that contingency over the decades, and there is almost complete consensus on the extreme unlikelihood that mere terrorists lacking the resources of a state could build such weapons themselves. Making even the simplest, cheapest nuclear weapon, even now when all the technical secrets are virtually out in the open, requires an investment of hundreds of millions of dollars, enough electrical power to run a fair-sized city, and access to rare and strictly controlled raw materials and precision machinery. Terrorists are not going to put one together in the garage – but in theory they might steal or be given one.

Anxiety that a nuclear weapon could fall into "the wrong hands" peaked in the few years after the collapse of the Soviet Union in 1991, when large numbers of warheads were left outside the borders of Russia in Ukraine, Belarus, and Kazakhstan, and the security and accounting procedures for nuclear weapons even inside Russia were very lax. By 1993–94, partly as a result of American assistance to the Russian authorities, all the weapons were back on Russian soil, security measures had dramatically improved, and none seemed to be missing. Nobody can be certain, of course, but if one or two nuclear warheads did "fall off the back of a truck" in the former Soviet Union in the early 1990s and end up in terrorist hands, we would probably know about it because the weapons would almost certainly have been used by now. What would be the point in waiting ten years?

The one remaining source of worry is that some "rogue state," as the U.S. State Department used to put it, might just give a nuclear weapon to a terrorist group. This concern is allegedly what drives American policy towards Iraq, and there is no doubt that Saddam Hussein spent many billion dollars over a period of more than a decade (1979–1991) in a determined attempt to build nuclear weapons, so it seems like a legitimate concern. But there are two important bits generally left out of the argument. *Why* did Saddam want nuclear weapons all that time ago, when America was still his friend and al-Qaeda was not even a glint in Osama bin Laden's eye? And how likely is it that he actually has them?

The theory of deterrence, sacred writ in American military circles for more than four decades, has taken a beating in the United States over the past few years as the advocates of "ballistic missile defence" shift to new rationalizations to justify their proposed new investments, but deterrence is still the basic intellectual framework for thinking about nuclear weapons. If a government has thousands of nuclear weapons, half a dozen different ways of delivering them, and stacks of money to play with, then it may be seduced by the endless schemes for making nuclear weapons "usable" that are dreamed up by the experts in the field: idle ingenuity, careerist ambition, and sheer boredom with the status quo play as large a role in nuclear strategy as in any other field. But if a government has just a few nuclear weapons, then it has to take its strategy seriously.

So let us consider Iraq, Iran, and North Korea, to pick three countries not entirely at random, and ask: What would just a few nuclear weapons be good for? Your measly few bombs won't let you take on a major nuclear-weapons power and win or even survive. But even a superpower will become a great deal more cautious and less arrogant if it cannot be sure of eliminating every one of your nuclear weapons in a surprise attack. Even if the superpower is certain of winning in the end, almost no policy goal is worth losing a city for.

This explains the great difference in American policy towards North Korea and Iraq, by the way. The United States has no intention of going to war with North Korea because Kim Jong Il is close to having deliverable nuclear weapons, if not actually there. In other words, he has effective deterrence. Washington has no reluctance about attacking Iraq because, despite their rhetoric, nobody in the Bush administration really believes that Saddam Hussein has a viable nuclear weapons program. When they talk about forcing Saddam to disarm and get rid of his weapons of mass destruction, they are playing with words, for the only WMD he might actually have are some old poison gas munitions left over from the Iran-Iraq War and perhaps a canister or two of liquid anthrax toxin: nasty, but not the end of the world. They know that most of the public doesn't understand the difference, however, and they don't go out of their way to help clear the confusion up. But let us stay with the subject of nuclear weapons, for "mushroom clouds" is what President Bush invokes to frighten Americans. Why would the members of the "axis of evil" want nuclear weapons anyway? Who are they afraid of?

The country that Iran and North Korea might hope to deter from a nuclear attack by the threat of nuclear retaliation, if only with a few weapons, is obviously the United States. The U.S. government has regularly denounced these regimes over decades, it is or has been effectively allied to their principal local enemies, Iraq and South Korea, and it has never prom-ised not to use its own nuclear weapons first. If Iran and North Korea did not have nuclear weapons programs, you would wonder why. Iraq is a different case, for during the years when its nuclear weapons program was most active and advanced, from the late 1970s to the beginning of the 1990s, it was not on any American hit list. Once Saddam Hussein invaded Iran in 1980, in fact, he was treated as a de facto ally by Washington. It was an uncomfortable alliance for the United States, which was well aware of Saddam's appalling human rights record in general and his extensive use of poison gas in particular. State Department types used to murmur wryly that "it's a pity both sides can't lose" – but if they couldn't both lose, then the United States was determined to ensure that it was Iran that lost. So who, in that case, was Saddam developing his bomb to deter? Israel, of course.

Saddam Hussein is a brutal and violent man, but he is not a cartoon villain. The Joker in the Batman comics has no real motives for what he does – he's just evil, that's all – but in real life people come from a particular context, and Saddam's formative experience was living through the 1950s, 1960s, and 1970s in the Middle East. He belongs to the generation of Arabs who made revolutions against Western control of their countries, fought against Israel, and tried to catch up with the developed world through copying the political dictatorship and command economies of the Soviet bloc. They largely failed in all three goals, but they still care, more or less – even Saddam. In the glory days of the Arab revolt against Western control, when puppet regimes like King Farouk in Egypt, King Idris in Libya, and King Faisal in Iraq were tumbling like tenpins, the great hero of this revolutionary generation was

Gamal Abdel Nasser, the Egyptian colonel who drove the British out, swore to defeat Israel, and even promised the unification of the Arab world. Saddam, who was born almost twenty years after Nasser, in 1937, and grew up under his spell, has always imagined that he might one day fill that kind of leadership role in the Arab world himself. Iraq is the wrong place to lead the Arab world from and Saddam is definitely the wrong man to lead it, but even thugs have dreams.

If you dream of uniting the Arab world behind you, there is only one subject that will do the trick. It's the same one that did it for Nasser: Israel. But Iraq doesn't even have a common land border with Israel, and besides it's been decades since any Arab state was bold and foolish enough to take Israel on in a war. Some of them have made peace, like Egypt and Jordan, and the rest have quietly abandoned the attempt to keep up with Israel militarily, because there's no point. Israel is incomparably the greatest military power of the region in conventional terms, and has beaten the Arabs in war five times; it has the unstinting support of the world's only superpower in almost everything it does; and, as if that weren't enough, it is the only nuclear power in the Middle East, with several hundred warheads and missiles able to deliver them on every major Arab city in less than half an hour. No wonder Arab governments appear paralyzed when they have to deal with anything involving Israel, and would really rather just change the subject.

But this humiliating paralysis of Arab governments creates an opportunity for an accomplished demagogue like Saddam Hussein: he doesn't really have to do much to look better than they do. Having a war with Israel would be foolish and probably suicidal, but what if he managed to break Israel's nuclear monopoly by creating an Arab nuclear deterrent? Just a few bombs, mind you, for Iraq could not hope to match Israel's large nuclear arsenal, and in any case Israel would attack Iraq pre-emptively if it felt seriously threatened. But even a few "Arab" nuclear weapons, provided they were kept safe from destruction in an Israeli surprise attack, would transform the strategic relationship between Israel and its neighbours, because it would no longer be able to destroy their great cities with no warning and complete impunity. The prize for Saddam in all this is that he would instantly become the hero and leader of the whole Arab world: a boyhood dream come true. In real life, it would probably all end in disaster, but he took it seriously enough to pour huge amounts of money into the project over many years.

In 1990, he may have been as little as two or three years away from manufacturing a crude nuclear weapon (which would have been much too big and heavy to put on a missile), but his defeat in the Gulf War ended all that. The UN arms inspectors were all over the country for the next eight years under the terms of the armistice agreement, and although Saddam's regime played a permanent game of hide-and-seek with them, it's quite clear that the vast majority of his nuclear weapons-related facilities had been dismantled or destroyed by the time the inspectors were withdrawn in 1998. Bits and pieces doubtless remained, but for the subsequent four years before the inspectors returned in November 2002 he continued to be under a very strict embargo. This would not have allowed him to get the nuclear program back up and running in a big way. In his post–September 11 report to Congress, George Tenet, director of the Central Intelligence Agency, wrote dismissively: "We believe that Iraq has probably continued at least low-level theoretical R&D associated with its nuclear program. A sufficient source of fissile material remains its most significant obstacle to being able to produce a nuclear weapon."

That, of course, was written before the current Bush administration decided to target Iraq. It remains true that no major intelligence agency believes that Iraq has nuclear weapons or is anywhere near having them, but the American intelligence services and those of its main ally, Britain, now find themselves under great pressure to publicly support the contrary position of their political masters. Even so, they manage to make their dissent clear. In Prime Minister Tony Blair's fifty-page dossier "Iraq's Weapons of Mass Destruction," submitted to the British parliament in September 2002, for example, there was a great deal of rhetoric about the threat from Iraqi weapons of mass destruction, but the key passage, distilled from reports submitted by the intelligence services, read as follows: "In early 2002 the Joint Intelligence Committee judged that . . . while UN sanctions on Iraq remain effective Iraq would not be able to produce a nuclear weapon. If they were removed or proved ineffective, it would take Iraq at least five years to produce sufficient fissile material for a weapon indigenously."

It's all smoke and mirrors: Saddam Hussein doesn't have any nuclear weapons, he wouldn't give them to terrorists if he did, and he has no plausible hope of ever getting any so long as he is under UN surveillance – which, in effect, was always going to be for life. He was successfully contained, and there was no need to have a war and kill lots of people in order to stop him. So if an administration in Washington wants to have a war anyway, and must get a democratic public and press on side or it won't happen, then it has to confuse the issue as much as possible. That is why Western audiences have been hearing so little from their leaders that is specifically about nuclear weapons (though the implication is always there that Saddam has nukes), and so much about that far vaguer category: weapons of mass destruction. At the time of writing, the ploy was still working, at least in the United States, where about half the population not only thought that Saddam Hussein had nuclear weapons but had also been tricked into believing that he was wholly or partly responsible for al-Qaeda's attacks on September 11. You can fool some of the people all of the time, and you can fool all of the people some of the time. . . .

. . . but why do they let themselves be fooled so easily? The agendas really driving the attack on Iraq are so transparent that it's hard to understand why the American media and a reasonably well-educated public have fallen into line so tamely. The administration of Bush the Elder had to struggle mightily with public opinion and a recalcitrant Congress to commit American troops to repel a blatant incursion in an area of clear American national interest, the Iraqi occupation of Kuwait in 1990. Twelve years later, Bush the Younger doesn't even have to produce any evidence of Iraqi misdeeds to get carte blanche to attack the place: the Congressional resolution of October 2002 simply grants him blanket authority "to use the armed forces of the United States as he determines to be necessary and appropriate in order to defend the national security of the United States against the continuing threat posed by Iraq." He didn't even have to invent a Gulf of Tonkin–style incident. What has happened to Americans' natural skepticism?

The answer is the extraordinary level of fear generated by the attacks on September 11, 2001. It's not that Americans are especially timid. Indeed, Americans habitually live with higher levels of personal insecurity in their day-to-day lives than the citizens of any other developed society: murder rates three or four times higher than in European countries, and practically no safety-net for the losers in the economy. It's partly a cultural matter – three centuries of an open frontier leaves its traces – and by now it's also an explicit ideological matter for many Americans: they consciously prefer a less regulated society even if it's also less equal and more dangerous. When it comes to the familiar danger of being murdered by a stranger who lives only five miles from you, Americans do not go into a collective funk: that's just part of the cost of the American way. It is when the danger is unfamiliar that people lose their nerve – and for Americans, *foreigners* trying to kill them at home in the United States is an unprecedented threat.

Geography plays a big role in this, because for at least a century and a half now it has been technologically impossible for any overseas country to invade the United States. Once moving troops on land by rail became faster than moving them across oceans by ship, it ceased to be feasible for European countries to ship armies across the Atlantic and land them successfully on American shores, as they had done so many times in the previous three centuries. As late as 1814, a British fleet sailed up Chesapeake Bay and landed an army that burned Washington long before the far larger numbers of American troops that were theoretically available could concentrate against it, since soldiers still marched on foot at less than a fifth of the speed of ships. By 1860, however, with a network of railways knitting together the whole American eastern seaboard, that simply wasn't possible any more: technology had made the United States invulnerable to transatlantic attack.

It was this knowledge that they couldn't really be successfully attacked at home that made it possible for Americans to follow George Washington's parting injunction to avoid entangling alliances for a full century. The main reason countries make alliances is because they fear attack, and on the whole Americans didn't. Even when the U.S. finally rejoined the old world of military alliances and great-power wars in 1917, it did so as a volunteer, not as just another country scrambling to protect itself. This was what gave Woodrow Wilson the moral leverage that enabled him to impose his grand plan for a League of Nations to keep the peace on his more cynical colleagues at the Paris Peace Conference in 1919.

This American sense of invulnerability was somewhat eroded by the Pearl Harbor attack in 1941, but the Hawaiian Islands are halfway across the Pacific and were not then even a state. Studs Terkel was able to title his book about Americans' experiences of the Second World War *The Good War* because it really *was* a good time for most Americans, who had good jobs and were safe at home. Apart from the millions of young soldiers who ended up fighting in Europe and the South Pacific, the war happened offstage for Americans – and that has continued to be the pattern down to the present. Television now brings the reality of war home far more vividly than before, so much so that people don't want to send their children off to deal with it, but for Americans war is still just pictures on a screen, not bombs on their houses or tanks in their streets.

By the 1950s, of course, intercontinental bombers and ballistic missiles finally put an end to America's century-long invulnerability to attack. But the threat of a nuclear war remained unreal and hypothetical to most Americans, who continued to believe "it can't happen here" through all the decades of debate about missile throw-weights, "Star Wars" defences, and extended deterrence. The citizens of London, Berlin, Moscow, and Tokyo know better (or at least they used to), for death has come out of the skies to all of those cities before. The citizens of New York should have known that they were not so much exempt as lucky for the moment, but the powerful tradition of American exceptionalism misled them into thinking that invulnerability was their birthright.

The terrorist attacks on New York and Washington therefore came out of nowhere as far as most Americans were concerned and fundamentally changed their perceptions of risk. The statistical reality hadn't changed all that much, but that is hardly relevant, for in matters of risk, perception is all: it's not uncommon these days in the United States to meet heavy smokers who worry about terrorism. Indeed, this pervasive sense of insecurity is what has let the current administration play the games it does with the American psyche. We have to do this to deal with the "terrorist threat," the administration says, and though most people doubt it, it, they are frightened. Besides, it is hard to be the one who stands up, says no, and breaks the consensus.

So there is going to be a war – not a very big one, if we are lucky, but that remains to be seen.

There is a pervasive illusion that Iraq 2003 will be a rerun of Kuwait 1991. It is related to the remarkable fact that George the son appears to be set on having a war with Saddam Hussein at the same time of year in roughly the same place as George the father. Therefore, many people assume, it will be the same sort of war, but that is not the case. This war will be quite different, and its course and outcome are not so predictable as in the first Gulf War. It is unlikely that many of America's Western allies will contribute significant numbers of troops, and it is almost certain that none of its Arab allies will. More importantly, the objective is different this time: not to drive the Iraqi occupying forces out of the small desert kingdom of Kuwait, but to bring about "regime change" in Iraq: that is, to overthrow Saddam Hussein and replace the Ba'athist ruling party with a government more favourable to American interests. But if you want to get Saddam Hussein, you have to go to Baghdad.

The part of the Gulf War that was actually fought was a "clean" war out in the desert, with almost no civilians around and no shelter for Iraqi troops, where the overwhelmingly superior firepower of the coalition forces and, above all, of the U.S. air force could have free rein. These were ideal conditions for the kind of war the U.S. armed forces prefer to fight. The bitter lessons of the Vietnam War continue to drive tactical doctrine and even procurement decisions in the Pentagon today: the first priority in U.S. military operations is always to minimize American casualties, in order not to alienate popular support for the war back home. The desperate situation of the Iraqi army in 1991, sitting in trenches far out in the desert and hundreds of miles from home, was tailor-made for this approach: American and allied air power and artillery killed tens of thousands of Iraqi troops in a methodical slaughter that they could not protect or defend themselves against, and the rest surrendered or fled. Only 148 American soldiers and 65 soldiers of the other coalition forces died.

But there was a second phase of the Gulf War that was not fought in 1991: the part where the victorious coalition forces sweep on up to Baghdad, where they kill or capture Saddam Hussein. One reason that part didn't happen was that the United States, in the course of persuading its Arab friends to supply troops and bases for the war, had promised that the fighting would stop once Kuwait had been liberated, but we should not imagine that America was bound with hoops of steel by this promise, nor indeed that the Arab allies would have minded all that much in private if Saddam Hussein could have been disposed of without too much mess. The problem, then and now, was the fact that it would probably be very messy.

As soon as Saddam Hussein realized in 1990 that he had made a ghastly mistake in invading Kuwait and that the United States was really going to fight to drive him out, he switched to survival mode. It was clearly impossible to hold Kuwait against an American attack, and he gradually thinned out his army there until most of the troops left to face the coalition onslaught were poorly trained and doubtfully loyal Kurdish and Shia conscripts. Most of the more reliable Sunni Arab troops, including the well-trained and well-paid Republican Guards divisions, were pulled back into the cities, above all into Baghdad. Iraq is heavily urbanized, and if Saddam were to survive an invasion he would have had to hold the cities: that was where revolts against his rule were most likely, but even more importantly the Americans would be deeply reluctant to come after him there. Street-fighting always means high casualties, and the U.S. armed forces would certainly have a professional preference for stopping with their cheap victory out in the desert, rather than going on to Baghdad and watching the casualty toll soar.

Saddam Hussein was right in 1991: Washington decided to quit while it was ahead. But now, twelve years later, the United States is going to do the second part of the war. It may not be a disaster, for the technology is even better twelve years on – but it could be, and you have to ask how we got here in less than two years without anything resembling a "smoking gun." Without assuming that they plotted out this exact course of events, you have to hand it to al-Qaeda. It appears to have fallen back into a secondary role at the moment thanks to the obsessive Washington focus on Iraq, but it was al-Qaeda that staged the event that started the avalanche moving. And it is al-Qaeda that stands to benefit most from the avalanche.

CHAPTER II

HUNTINGTON'S FOLLY
(AND BIN LADEN'S)

"The nations of infidels have all united against Muslims. . . . This is a new battle, a great battle, similar to the great battles of Islam like the conquest of Jerusalem. . . . [The Americans] come out to fight Islam in the name of fighting terrorism. These events have split the whole world into two camps: the camps of belief and the camps of disbelief. . . ."

– Osama bin Laden, early October 2001

B	in Laden's video message to the Muslim world, pre-
taped for release after the first U.S. strikes against
Afghanistan in October 2001, must have given Samuel
Huntington a warm glow of satisfaction, for it was he who
predicted in his best-selling 1995 book *The Coming Clash of
Civilizations* that Islam and the West would become global
adversaries. Huntington's book was especially popular among
the Washington-based professionals who had built lucrative
careers on fighting the Soviet threat, and by the early 1990s
were desperately in need of a new threat to replace it. So
bearded fanatics took the place of godless commissars – but to
be fair to Huntington, he was just predicting the phenomenon,
not advocating it.

Islamists like bin Laden, on the other hand, already believed
that contemporary history is a morality play in which the
oppressed and despised peoples of the Muslim world were des-
tined to unite, wage a final battle against "Western civilization,"
and overthrow its domination throughout the world. This is
the worldview that bin Laden pushes relentlessly every time he
finds a camera to address, and he is quite prepared to give
history a shove in that direction. The current crisis will give this

definition of the world a big boost in both of the civilizations in question, yet it remains pure parochial nonsense. There is no clash of civilizations, only a clash between traditionalists and modernizers *within* each culture, religion, and civilization.

The battle between reformers and conservatives began in the West more than five hundred years ago, long before it began in other parts of the planet, but it is at least a century old in most Muslim societies. As in other non-Western cultures, the defenders of the old ways in Muslim countries find it is always a good tactic to portray their modernizing opponents at home as mere pawns of a foreign cultural invasion – and, in most cases, to fix on the United States as the symbolic "aggressor" who is forcing modernism down their throats. There is a certain irony in this, as the United States in some respects is a rather old-fashioned place. It remains a profoundly religious country – American politicians invoke God just as often as Iranian or Afghan ones do – whereas in most other developed countries religion is a private and marginal matter. Indeed, the United States is the only country in the West where there is an ongoing and evenly balanced "culture war" between secular modernists and religious conservatives, which parallels the struggle in so many Third World countries. Never mind: those who are committed to the struggle against modernism need an external enemy, and the United States is their obvious choice.

It's commonplace for the defenders of tradition to speak of the struggle in the most cataclysmic moral terms – as a pro-Taliban youth in an Afghan refugee camp in Pakistan put it recently: "The Americans love Coca-Cola, but we love death" –

but it would be an error to see this as a particularly Islamic response. A Japanese kamikaze pilot in 1945 could have said it with equal sincerity. Every major culture on the planet is at some stage or other of working its way through the same series of changes, collectively called modernization, that follows on the heels of mass urbanization, mass education, and mass communications. Occasionally those who abhor the whole process win out, at least for a while, and when it happens in a great power, like Japan in the 1930s, great upheavals may ensue. When it happens in less powerful countries, like Iran since the late 1970s or, perhaps, some Arab countries in the near future, the repercussions are more modest (though still painful close up). But it is going to happen from time to time, and in this historical epoch the United States, as the most powerful of the Western countries, is going to be the designated Great Satan.

The nineteen terrorists who flew planes into the World Trade Center and the Pentagon were fanatics who had cut loose from normal human concepts of good and evil, and what they did was a monstrous crime – but they were not *stupid*. Hijacking four commercial airliners within a few minutes of each other, using no weapon bigger than a box-cutter, and successfully flying three of them into relatively small and hard-to-hit targets hundreds of miles away required a high level of organization and discipline. The hijackers were driven by hatred, but it was not blind hatred.

People capable of formulating and carrying out this plan were also intelligent enough to consider what the United

States would do in response to it. Indeed, it's a reasonable assumption that the attacks were designed to elicit some specific reaction from the United States. The attacks may have been partly about raising the profile of al-Qaeda in the Muslim world, or just killing Americans in order to please God, but this operation engaged the energies of several dozen people for up to three years: it was not undertaken out of mere anger and hunger for publicity. For the planners and leaders, if not for all the foot soldiers who carried out the actual hijackings, there must have been a strategy. What was it?

It is axiomatic in the terrorist trade never to discuss your real strategy. (It's pretty standard operating procedure in the mainstream political trade too.) Terrorists often wax eloquent about their goals and ideals, but they almost never talk about the cold and often convoluted calculations they make about how their actions will get them closer to those goals. There is a specific technical reason for this: terrorist strategies wither when exposed to the full light of day, because the very people they seek to manipulate would not respond in the desired way if they understood how the terrorists seek to direct their emotions and reactions by inflicting horrors upon them.

So we need to understand al-Qaeda's strategy, but we cannot expect the organization's spokespersons to enlighten us on the subject directly. Instead, we must figure out what the hijackers hoped to achieve by looking at who they were and what kind of organization they belonged to. The answer is that they were all Arabs, and that they were all associated with al-Qaeda, an organization that claims to be pan-Islamic but is in practice overwhelmingly Arab in membership. Could this be about the Middle East, then?

The Arab as opposed to Muslim character of the hijack teams and the organization behind them cannot be stressed too much. They were devout followers of an extreme Islamic sect who claimed to be acting on behalf of Muslims everywhere. But the point is that Arabs are only about a fifth of the world's Muslim population; *all* of the people involved in planning and carrying out the attacks were Arabs. So it is in Arab politics, not in some misty Hegelian concept of a coming clash of civilizations, that we should look for the answers.

The relationship of the Arab world to the broader Muslim world is rather like that of Europe to the broader Christian world: it is in many ways the ancestral culture to the larger whole, but in no serious sense is it the leader of a united community. Americans, Bolivians, and to some extent even Filipinos may acknowledge that they have a European heritage, but that does not mean they think as Europe thinks, let alone fight when Europe fights. The emotional bond that other Muslims feel they have with the Arabs is perhaps stronger than that of other Christians towards Europeans, because Muhammad himself was an Arab and the holy places of Islam are still in the Arab world, whereas the original holy places of Christianity are all in the Middle East and have not been under Christian rule for most of the past thirteen centuries. But never in history have non-Arab Muslims gone to war to protect Arab interests, and they are not going to start now. Moreover, and very much to the point, the Arab fifth of the

Islamic world has had a much more bitter experience at the hands of the West over most of the past century than the other four-fifths.

Bernard Lewis, professor emeritus at Princeton University, recently wrote a book about the astonishing collapse of Muslim power, influence, and confidence over the past few centuries and called it simply *What Went Wrong?* No Muslim reader would need a subtitle, for it is a theme that resonates in every predominantly Muslim society. But for most of the larger Muslim countries, the worst is past.

The Muslims of Asia lost a great deal because of European imperial rule in the past – above all in the British destruction of Muslim hegemony in the Indian subcontinent – but it all ended half a century ago with decolonization. Some Asian Muslim countries have done quite well since then, and some have done badly, but neither outcome owes much to Western influence. Much the same is true of the partly Muslim countries of sub-Saharan Africa. The Turks, who were a European great power until 1918 and escaped colonization entirely, have a relatively small chip on their shoulder about Europe. Iranians are probably closest to the Arabs in the bitterness they feel about recent Western insults to their dignity and attacks on their prosperity and freedoms, but as Iranians are Shia Muslims and Arabs are overwhelmingly Sunni, this has not led to any alliance between them.

No, the Arabs are mostly on their own in this, and they are very bitter indeed. They are a people with a long and glorious history behind them – a thousand years ago, they were probably the leading civilization on the planet – and they have a correspondingly high opinion of themselves, but things have been going wrong for them for a long time now. They languished for hundreds of years under Ottoman Turkish rule, still revered as the original bearers of Islam but regarded by most Turkish administrators as near-savages. (Turkish slang for a hopeless mess is *Arap saçı* – Arab hair.) Then they passed without any interval of independence into various European empires, British, French, and Italian, a process that was complete by 1918 and effectively lasted until after the Second World War. While European rule was no worse than Turkish, it was much more humiliating because this was the first time since the Crusades nine hundred years earlier that the founding people of Islam had fallen under non-Muslim rule.

It was the greatest shock that the Arabs had suffered in centuries, and it produced in due course a generation of passionate Arab nationalists who were determined to expel the Europeans and restore the Arab peoples to their proper place in the world. They succeeded in their first aim, but not in their second. All the Arab countries had regained their independence by the early 1960s, a few, like Algeria, after bitter independence wars, but most without serious fighting. However, they failed utterly in their attempt to modernize and catch up with the West.

The modernizers who came to power in most of the bigger Arab countries in the two decades after Gamal Abdel Nasser's coup in Egypt in 1952 were young, predominantly from military backgrounds – and unanimously convinced that rapid economic growth would best be achieved by copying the Eastern European socialist style. (Bizarre though this may now seem, the Communist command economies actually grew faster than Western economies from the 1930s to the 1960s, which was the period the Arab reformers had available as evidence – and of course they were attracted to the "command" aspect of the system as well.) Given the almost universal failure of the state socialist system in so-called Third World countries, and what subsequently happened in the industrialized Communist countries as well, it's unlikely that this approach to the problem of catching up would ever have worked for the Arab countries. What made matters far worse for the Arabs, however, was the creation of Israel in 1948.

Israel has had three impacts on the Arab world. The first is a deep resentment that the West, rather than doing penance and giving compensation for the massacre of the European Jews at its own expense, chose to make the Arabs pay the price instead. The second is profound humiliation and despair at the fact that all their wars against Israel have ended in defeat: there are almost 300 million Arabs in the Middle East compared to only about 5 million Jews in Israel, and yet after five wars over fifty years, Israel has gone from being a beleaguered enclave to the local superpower, controlling far more territory than it did in 1948 and possessing an absolute military superiority over all its neighbours. The third is that the Arab defeats, far from causing the overthrow of the regimes that were responsible for them, have frozen the entire Arab world in the patterns of the past.

Apart from Fidel Castro's forty-two-year-old regime in Cuba, there is no government in all of the Americas that has been in power for more than fifteen years, and few that have been there for more than ten. The same is true of Europe, and largely true for Asia as well. (The exceptions are the four surviving Communist countries, China, North Korea, Vietnam, and Laos, plus Burma and a few mini-states.) Even in sub-Saharan Africa, at least half the countries have seen a major change of political leadership in the past ten years. But in the Arab world, there is virtual stasis: out of eighteen Arab countries, only three have seen real political change in the past thirty years. In all three cases – Sudan, Lebanon, and Yemen – the changes were the result of civil wars. Apart from that, nothing.

The great majority of the countries in the Arab world are ruled either by those same statist, mostly military modernizers of thirty or forty years ago or by their lineal descendants – the Algerian military regime, Muammar Gaddafi in Libya, Hosni Mubarak in Egypt, Bashar al-Assad (the Younger) in Syria, Saddam Hussein in Iraq – or else by absolute monarchies that survived the wave of revolutions that swept away so many other Arab kings in the 1950s and 1960s: the Hashemite family in Jordan, the Saudi family in Arabia, the Sabah family in Kuwait, and so on. There is not a single genuine and full democracy in the Arab world, and only a few countries (Jordan, Lebanon, Morocco, and Qatar) that even try to look like democracies.

Whether they are military regimes, single-party dictator-ships, or traditional monarchies, most Arab governments are deeply corrupt, very long in the tooth, and almost completely discredited by their abject failure to deliver either victory against Israel or economic growth at home. Living standards have been falling steeply in the Arab world for a generation now, as populations have risen and economies failed to grow: in Saudi Arabia, average per capita income has fallen by two-thirds from its 1980 peak, and in non-oil countries, which never got rich, the plight of the poor is appalling. Half of all Arab women are illiterate; science and technology are as com-atose as intellectual life; censorship is everywhere and free media were practically non-existent until the recent advent of television channels broadcasting directly from satellites. It is as much a testimony to the sheer disabling despair that paralyzes Arab societies as to the efficiency of their secret police forces that these regimes have lasted so long without being toppled by the citizens who despise and hate them.

These startling political and economic failures are an *Arab* phenomenon, not a general Muslim one. A majority of the world's non-Arab Muslims live in more or less democratic countries, and some of those countries are doing a creditable job of digging themselves out of poverty. Turks, Bangladeshis, Malays, and Indonesians all have their quarrels with the West, but nothing that couldn't be fixed with soft words and an even break. But the sense of failure and alienation in the Arab world is enormous: desperation drives, and the search for a solution, some magic nostrum that can rescue the Arabs from their century of defeat and humiliation, grows less discriminating as saner and more plausible remedies fail.

Islamic revivalism as a remedy for a real-world losing streak is not a new phenomenon in Muslim countries. There have always been various mystical sects in Islam, as there are also in its sister religions, Judaism and Christianity, and occasionally, as with the Mahdi in late nineteenth-century Sudan, they have acquired serious military and political power. Mainstream, non-mystical Islam and Christianity also share a propensity for spawning extreme puritanical, male-centred sects whose program for winning heavenly approval and earthly dominion revolves around banning everything that is merely pleasant, pretty, or frivolous. One such sect, arising in northern Arabia in the nineteenth century, was Wahhabism, which provided the ideological fuel for the armies that created Saudi Arabia and remains the state-approved form of Islam in the kingdom today. Then there are the perennial, cynical attempts by beleaguered governments of multi-ethnic states to enlist Islam as a unifying factor, from the Young Turks in the dying days of the Ottoman Empire to the secular governments of Iraq and Pakistan today.

The state-sponsored revivals don't count for much. The mystical sects come and go at a very stately pace – a lifespan of centuries, usually – but rarely have much impact on the ways of the secular world. Puritanical currents within mainstream Sunni Islam have great political potential in principle, but during the middle decades of the twentieth century they were largely crowded out by the many secular schemes for salvation, most of them socialist and authoritarian, that were being promoted throughout the Arab world. It was only as the secular solutions failed and the regimes peddling them calcified into self-serving dictatorships, like that of the Assad dynasty in Syria, that solutions based on religion became attractive. The watershed date for the rapid rise of political Islam is probably 1967, the year of the Arabs' most catastrophic military defeat at the hands of Israel, but the modern doctrine of militant Islamism had begun to take shape several decades earlier.

In 1948, a forty-two-year-old Egyptian novelist, poet, and critic named Sayyid Qutb sailed from Alexandria for New York on his first visit to the West. He spent two years in the United States at the expense of King Farouk's government, and was revolted by what he saw. A puritanical man and a lifelong bachelor, he viewed the relatively permissive culture of post–Second World War America as a bottomless sink of moral iniquity, with temptations waiting to trap the believer at every turn. Even a harmless church hop dismayed him with what he saw as flagrant sexuality: in one of his letters from America he recounts how the pastor put on a record of "Baby, It's Cold Outside" and "The dancing intensified. . . . The hall swarmed with legs. . . . Arms circled arms, lips met lips, chests met chests, and the atmosphere was full of love."

Qutb's sensibility, if not his strategy, prefigured almost precisely that of Mohammed Atta, chief of the September 11 hijackers, and of a whole later generation of other lonely, socially awkward young Muslim men in the diaspora who were simultaneously fascinated and terrified by the sexual openness of the modern West and took refuge in a pose of fastidious disengagement from the corruption around them. As Qutb later described it, "The Believer from his height looks down at the people drowning in dirt and mud. He may be the only one; yet he is not dejected or grieved, nor does his heart desire that he take off his clean and immaculate garments and join the crowd." And not long after he got home to Egypt in 1950, he joined the Muslim Brotherhood.

The philosophy that Qutb developed over the next decade, codified in his 1964 book *Milestones*, built on the Salafi tradition in Islam. The name comes from al-Salaf al-Salih, "the venerable forefathers," a reference to the generation of the Prophet and his companions, and the Salafis hold that most modern Muslims are little more than idolaters and must strive to return Islamic society to the pure state of that first generation of Muslims, fourteen centuries ago. Qutb's special contribution, and the key to his doctrine's immense influence in the Arab world over the succeeding decades, was to make an explicit analogy between the current dreadful state of the Arab world (he would have said Islamic world, but the only part he really knew was the Middle East) and the evil state of things in seventh-century Arabia in the decades before the Prophet's birth: foreign occupation, sin, vulgarity, and ignorance. The pre-Islamic period is known in Arabic as the jahiliyah (literally, "the state of ignorance"), and Qutb declared that the Arab world had fallen victim to a new jahiliyah from which only religious reform could save it.

But while the language was Koranic, Qutb's thinking on how the jahiliyah might be ended borrowed very heavily from contemporary European ideologies, especially in adopting the notion of a revolutionary vanguard of militant believers who would bring about this transformation by violence. As Malise Ruthven noted in his book *A Fury for God*, this is a concept "imported from Europe, through a lineage that stretches back to the Jacobins, through the Bolsheviks and latter-day Marxist guerillas such as the Baader-Meinhof gang." So it's hardly surprising that Nasser had Qutb executed in 1966 – but his martyrdom, coming only a year before the 1967 defeat discredited all the secular regimes of the Arab world, only gave his ideas added power.

It was the abject failure of the Arab nationalist and Marxist regimes to solve the two great problems of the Arab world – Israel and backwardness – that caused many people to turn to militant Islamism in the 1970s. As early as 1972, according to recently opened records, the British Foreign Office was picking up signs that Islamic radicalism was beginning to take over as the dominant revolutionary movement in the Arab world. That was the year that diplomat James Craig, later British ambassador to Syria and Saudi Arabia, wrote in a memorandum after a visit to several Arab countries, "One theory put to me in Beirut was that, since Arab nationalism had manifestly failed, people are turning to the alternative of Islamic nationalism. I argued that this, too, had failed – indeed, it failed long ago. The reply was that the very length of time which had passed since this failure made it possible to consider giving it a second trial run."

There was, however, a serious ideological problem that the Salafis had to solve if their ideas were to command a mass following in the Arab world. Their ultimate goal was not nationalist at all: it was the establishment of a single transnational community of the faithful everywhere – the traditional idea of the umma – living under Sharia law in obedience to the original precepts of the founding generation of Islam as they conceived them. Nationalism, they believed, was an idolatry that only served to divide the umma, and ultimately all national boundaries should be erased. Most of their potential followers, however, were Arabs who were mainly concerned with the failures of existing Arab states in the here-and-now, and what they really wanted was better social and economic conditions, a restoration of Arab dignity, and if possible victory over Israel. Like the internationalist Bolsheviks who had to come to terms with the fact that their main clientele was nationalist Russians, the Islamists had to tailor their ideas to appeal to the interests and priorities of Arabs who were still primarily nationalists.

The solution was to argue that all the trials and defeats of this era, the darkest in the history of the Muslim peoples (of the Arabs, really, but slide past that), were due to a vast global plot hatched by the "Zionist-Crusader alliance" to enslave the Muslims and destroy Islam. Israel and the various Arab governments that co-operated with the West were all part of this plot, whose headquarters was in the United States. Therefore the things that really preoccupied the Arab man in the street – the struggle against Israel and the need to replace corrupt, incompetent, and repressive Arab governments – were legitimate and necessary parts of the larger struggle to defend and reform Islam. The real enemy was the West – and no one talked too much about the final goal of a single, all-embracing, and ultimately global Islamic state for the moment.

That was the high ideology of it. For the average Arab, the argument was a good deal simpler. Stripped to its bare bones, the logic goes like this: We Arabs have enjoyed God's favour from the time of the Prophet, and our history was mostly gloriously successful, but for generations now we have been losing every time, on every issue. What are we doing wrong that has made God turn away from us? If you ask this question anywhere in the Arab world these days, you will find somebody nearby with the answer: "We are doing everything wrong. For most of a century we have been trying to catch up with the West by *copying* the West – not just its technology, but its systems, its manners, its values, even its clothes. We have abandoned our own Islamic values and traditions, and so God has turned his back on us."

Not only is this argument internally consistent for the true believer, but it is immensely attractive because it implicitly promises that a solution is available. There is no need to beat the West at its own games, political, military, and economic (which is a great relief since we Arabs haven't been doing too well in that endeavour). On the contrary, what we must do is to abandon all these Westernized ways of thinking and acting, and return to our own Islamic values and behaviour. In other words, the solution is well within the reach of ordinary Arab men and women: we must only persuade all our fellow Muslims to return to the original and proper Islamic ways, and God will be with us once again. Then He will give us the power to overthrow the hated domination of the West, and we will resume our rightful place in the world.

The fly in this ointment is that relatively few people in any Arab country actually want to lead the extremely austere and in many ways pre-modern lives that the Islamists insist is the only proper way to live Islam. Yet that is what everybody must do if the Islamists' solution is to work – so the reluctant majority must be forced into the proper ways, which requires that the Islamists gain control of the state, pass laws that define proper Islamic comportment, and enforce them against the entire population. To be an Islamist is to be a revolutionary, and from the beginning the organizations they created in the various Arab states were precisely that. During the 1970s such groups as the Muslim Brotherhood in Syria and Takfir wal-Hijra in Egypt grew rapidly but remained out of sight – but at the end of the decade they came out into the open with a bang.

In November 1979, several hundred men led by Juhayman al-Utaybi, a veteran of the Saudi Arabian National Guard, seized control of the Grand Mosque in Mecca and proclaimed al-Utaybi's brother-in-law Muhammad al-Qahtani to be the Mahdi, the long-awaited messiah who, according to one tradition, would purify the Muslim world and lead the Muslims to victory. The Saudi rulers, al-Utaybi proclaimed, were apostates who had "made religion into a means of acquiring their materialistic interests. They have brought upon Muslims all evil and corruption." The Saudi government was at a loss as to how to respond, since the use of heavy weapons to retake Islam's most sacred site was out of the question, so they called on the help of the French gendarmerie's paramilitary anti-terrorism force, the Groupe d'Intervention.

It took them more than two weeks to take the mosque back in bitter hand-to-hand fighting, and rumours continue to circulate that poison gas was used, or that the mosque's basements were flooded and a high-voltage current passed through the water to electrocute the rebels. In the end al-Utaybi and more than sixty of his followers were captured and subsequently beheaded in the largest mass decapitation in Saudi history. And that was just the start.

In 1981, Islamist soldiers serving in the Egyptian army shot and killed President Anwar Sadat for having made peace with Israel. His successor, Hosni Mubarak, an ex-fighter pilot, has survived at least five Islamist assassination attempts. In 1983, the Muslim Brotherhood rose against Hafez al-Assad's Ba'athist regime in Syria, which was closely modelled on that of East Germany (except that it was mainly based on clan ties among the country's small Alawite minority), and seized control of the country's third largest city, Hama. The Syrian army took the city back with heavy artillery, killing an estimated twenty thousand people in the process. By the end of the 1980s, there were serious Islamist revolutionary organizations in all of the larger Arab countries that were perfectly willing to use violence in order to take power, so that they could begin to put their program for solving the Arab world's problems into effect.

The 1980s were the heyday of militant Islamism in the Arab world, a time when there were real fears that these radical anti-Western revolutionaries might actually gain power in a major Arab country (as their unacknowledged Shia cousins had done in Iran in 1978). They very nearly did achieve that goal in 1991 in Algeria, when the worn-out and totally discredited National Liberation Front (FLN) regime that has ruled that country since the French army pulled out in 1962 made the mistake of holding more or less free elections. "Le pouvoir," as the shadowy group of generals who actually run Algeria are known, believed they could control the outcome of the election and gain some legitimacy as a result. The first round of the parliamentary elections proved them wrong. Algerians would probably even have voted for the Gay Liberation Front if it seemed to have a chance of removing those in power, but the actual alternative they had was the Islamic Salvation Front (FIS), and they voted for it in droves. So the regime panicked and cancelled the second round of the elections.

France and the United States, which were appalled by the prospect of an Islamist government coming to power in Algeria, backed the ruling generals all the way. It was embarrassing for them to support publicly such a blatant rejection of democracy, but the alternative of an overtly Islamist government in what was, after all, the second most populous Arabic-speaking country (and an oil exporter, to boot) outweighed all other considerations. Algeria has paid a terrible price for this decision, as the thwarted Islamists then turned to violence. Between one and two hundred thousand people have been killed in a no-quarter war between the regime and the insurgents of the Armed Islamic Groups (GIA), FIS's armed wing, over the past decade – but it was, in the end, a defeat for the Islamists.

In fact, the crest of the Islamist wave seemed to have passed in the Arab world by the mid-1990s. The Islamists were still convinced that they had the solution, if only they could take power and put it into effect, but in fifteen years of trying they had had no success whatever. They had killed a great many people, and thousands of the Islamists themselves had died terrible deaths in the torture chambers of the regimes they were trying to overthrow, but they had nothing at all to show for it: no Arab state was ruled by Islamists, or seemed even close to falling into their hands. The cause was becoming just one more failure in the pattern of failure that had descended on the Arab world like an ancient curse. It was at this point that Osama bin Laden entered the scene.

"To the peoples of the countries allied to the iniquitous American government . . ." began the audiotape of November 2002 that gave the first clear evidence since the saturation bombing of the caves of Tora Bora in the White Mountains of southeastern Afghanistan the previous year that Osama bin Laden was still alive. "What has happened since the conquests of New York and Washington up until now – like the opera-tions on Germans in Tunisia, the explosion of the French tanker in Yemen, on the French in Karachi, the operations against the [U.S.] Marines in Failaka [Kuwait], on Australians and Britons in the explosions in Bali, as well as the recent hostage-taking in Moscow and other operations here and there – were nothing but the response of Muslims eager to defend their religion and respond to the order of God and their Prophet.

"What Bush, the pharaoh of the century, did by murdering our children in Iraq and what Israel, the ally of America, did in bombing the houses of the elderly, women, and children in Palestine, using American planes, was enough for the wise among your leaders to distance themselves from this criminal gang. . . . Do your governments not know that the clique in the White House is made up of the greatest murderers of the century? Rumsfeld is the butcher of Vietnam who has killed more than two million people. Cheney and Powell have murdered and destroyed in Baghdad more than did Hulagu [the thirteenth-century Mongol who conquered the city]. Why did your governments ally themselves with America to attack us in Afghanistan, and I cite in particular Great Britain, France, Italy, Canada, Germany and Australia? . . .

"[R]emember our [people] killed among the children of Palestine, in Iraq. Remember our dead in Afghanistan. As you look at your dead in Moscow, also recall ours in Chechnya. For how long will fear, massacres, destruction, exile, orphanhood and widowhood be our lot, while security, stability and joy remain your domain alone? It is high time that equality be established to this effect. As you assassinate, so will you be [assassinated], and as you bomb, so will you likewise be [bombed]."

In the dark arts of image management and political spin, Osama bin Laden could rope, pin, and hogtie President Bush's political manager and resident Machiavelli, Karl Rove, in under ten seconds. He sometimes affects sheikly robes to which he has no rightful claim (his father grew wealthy in the construction trade, but was of an undistinguished lineage), but in his carefully produced video appearances he more commonly wears a calculated mix of modern combat fatigues and the long beard and headdress of a traditional Islamic sage. And he regularly implies that events as widely separated as the Chechen attacks in Moscow and Palestinian bombings in Israel are all part of the same universal Muslim struggle against the "Zionist-Crusader alliance," and that his own organization and strategy are the solution.

What he wants, in other words, is to make Samuel Huntington's prediction of an apocalyptic clash of civilizations come to pass, and to portray what is really an Arab cause and organization as a pan-Islamic one. But the figures speak for themselves: al-Qaeda members in Afghanistan with bin Laden before September 2001, according to a series of interviews conducted with the Islamist leader by Ahmed Zeidan, al-Jazeera television's Islamabad correspondent, and later published as *Bin Laden Unmasked*, included 62 British Muslims, 30 Americans, 8 Frenchmen, 1,660 men from the Maghreb (Algeria, Morocco, and Tunisia), 680 Saudi Arabians, 480 Yemenis, 430 Palestinians, 270 Egyptians, 520 Sudanese, 80 Iraqis, 33 Turks and 180 Filipinos. There must have been substantial numbers of Afghan and Pakistani members as well, who are perhaps omitted because they had not travelled long distances to join bin Laden, but the statistics are still striking. While more than 80 per cent of the world's Muslims are non-Arabs, the overwhelming majority of al-Qaeda's combatants were from the Arab world.

It should also be noted that nearly a third of al-Qaeda's "Afghan Arabs" came from the Maghreb – principally from Algeria, where the bloody ten-year war between Islamist guerillas and the military regime has radicalized many young Muslims. One in seven came from Saudi Arabia, where the ruling family has long subsidized a network of Islamic colleges to keep the huge numbers of educated but unemployed youths off the streets. Less than a fifth came from the densely populated cultural heartland of the Arab world, the Fertile Crescent stretching from Egypt to Iraq that accounts for more than 40 per cent of the total Arab population – and only 2 per cent were Iraqis. Al-Qaeda isn't even representative of the Arab world, let alone of the broader Muslim world – but it has done a pretty good job of fooling the West in that regard.

Osama bin Laden was born in 1957 in Riyadh, Saudi Arabia, one of the youngest of the fifty-four children of Muhammad bin Laden, who was illiterate when he emigrated from Yemen in the 1930s but built up an enormous construction conglomerate in the Saudi kingdom, married eleven times – though never more than four wives at once – and was at one time the minister of public works (which is never bad for business). Unlike most of his family, Osama bin Laden never lived abroad and seems to have travelled only rarely, but surprisingly little is known about his youth. He first attracted public attention when, still in his twenties, he became one of the many Arab volunteers helping their fellow Muslims in Afghanistan to resist the Soviet occupation of that country.

The Soviet army entered Afghanistan in 1979 because it was worried that the beleaguered Marxist military regime in Kabul would fall. To get the necessary invitation to send its troops into Afghanistan, the Kremlin engineered a coup within that regime, so it is legitimate to say that the Russians invaded the country even though there was no official resistance. But the reason the pro-Moscow regime was teetering on the brink of collapse was the large amounts of clandestine arms and money the United States was providing to various opposition groups, most of them Islamists, who were unhappy at the Kabul regime's ideas about educating girls, redistributing land, and generally upsetting the established rural social order. And why was the U.S. backing these champions of feudal values?

If we are to believe former president Carter's national security adviser in the late 1970s, Zbigniew Brzezinski, it was precisely to force the Russians into direct military intervention to save the Kabul regime, and thereby draw them into a quagmire. On the day Soviet troops crossed the border into Afghanistan, he wrote to Carter, saying, "We now have the opportunity to give the U.S.S.R. their Vietnam war." So the Soviet armed forces plunged in, and the U.S. channelled ever greater amounts of military and financial aid to the rebels (who called themselves mujahedin, those who fight a jihad). After ten years, fifteen thousand dead, and thirty times that number of soldiers evacuated sick or injured, the Russians pulled out again, so it was an American victory – but by then the country was effectively destroyed.

Although Afghans are not Arabs and have little by way of recent shared history, many Arabs of an Islamist bent were moved by ties of common religion to help Afghanistan in various ways, and bin Laden was among them. His role for much of the ten-year struggle was that of a benevolent rich kid, using his own considerable wealth and his extensive contacts among Saudi élite families to provide aid to the mujahedin from an office in Peshawar in Pakistan's North-West Frontier Province, but towards the end he did fight with distinction himself in at least one battle against the Russians at Ali Khel in Paktia Province. He grew up in the Afghan war, coming into close and constant contact with Islamist radicals and becoming far more radical himself. For the United States, the "Afghan Arabs" were just useful proxy troops in the Cold War – as bin Laden said later, "The weapons were supplied by the Americans, the money by the Saudis" – but they became a force in their own right. Indeed, it was in Afghanistan in 1989, in the euphoric aftermath of victory over the Soviets, that he laid the foundations of al-Qaeda.

Over a period of little more than a decade, al-Quaeda has become paramount among Arab groups waging the Islamist struggle, and lays claim to influence over comparable groups throughout the Muslim world. It's hard to know what bin Laden intended it to become at that early stage in the organization's existence, but what it has evolved into is a kind of resource centre for strategic planning for the revolutionary Islamist movement. The Islamists desperately needed one by the early 1990s, for despite over a decade of trying and many thousands of deaths, they had failed to crack the problem of the end-game anywhere. They had not succeeded in taking power in even one Arab country.

Revolutionary movements seeking to overthrow an established government with its vast apparatus of military and police must either subvert the security forces or persuade huge numbers of people to join a popular uprising that sweeps the existing regime away, and the Islamists could do neither. Their strictures against the West and against corrupt and oppressive Arab regimes commanded a degree of public sympathy in most countries, but only a tiny minority of people shared their dream of a borderless Islamic superstate. Most people were cowed by the security forces, and a great many more were deeply unenthusiastic about the prospect of living under the austere rule of fanatics. A popular uprising that would bring the Islamists to power, therefore, was not very likely. As for subverting the security forces, the revolutionaries were almost completely unsuccessful in winning support among the officer corps of the various Arab armies, whose privileges were linked to the existing regimes. And the Islamists themselves were divided into a few large organizations and many small splinter groups, almost none of which extended beyond the borders of a single Arab state.

The result was a stalemate in which various Islamist groups from time to time carried out terrorist attacks against the organs of government or even against Western interests and visitors in the Arab world. In turn they were hunted down, tortured, and killed by the security apparatus of the various Arab governments. All the while the mass of the Arab population essentially sat on the fence, neither loving nor trusting either side in the conflict. What the Islamist cause needed was some sort of umbrella organization that linked up all the separate radical groups, co-ordinated their activities as much as possible, and did some serious strategic thinking about ways of breaking the stalemate, and that was what bin Laden set out to create. He quickly gave up on Afghanistan as a base, as the various mujahedin groups there descended into a brutal civil war after the departure of the Russians, and by the end of 1989 he was back in Saudi Arabia – just in time for Saddam Hussein's invasion of Kuwait in August 1990.

Bin Laden loathed the Iraqi regime, a textbook example of the kind of secular, socialist dictatorship he held responsible for the disasters that had befallen the Arab world, and he was already publicly advocating the overthrow of Saddam Hussein. Though he regarded the Saudi ruling family as apostates too – conservative and superficially Islamic in their domestic policies, but sold out to the West – it has been plausibly reported that in 1990 he privately offered to make his "Afghan Arab" veterans available for the defence of Saudi Arabia from the Iraqi threat. When the Saudi regime preferred realism and invited American troops in to protect the country instead, bin Laden was totally outraged, and he was not alone. Not just Islamists but many other Muslims interpret the tradition which says that the Prophet declared on his deathbed, "There shall be no two religions in Arabia" to mean an absolute ban on non-Muslim troops in the country, and the Saudis' decision to let U.S. forces in caused widespread dismay and significant popular protest in the kingdom.

For bin Laden, it was the last straw, and his open condemnation of the Saudi regime led to his expulsion in mid-1991 (and later to the cancellation of his citizenship). He found refuge in Sudan, where a leading Islamist scholar-politician, Hassan al-Turabi, had come to power in an alliance with a military officer, General Omar al-Bashir. Sudan is only partly an Arab country: about a third of the population, in the south, is ethnically African, mostly Christian or animist in religion, and almost permanently in revolt. The ongoing north-south civil war and the need to share power with the army prevented Turabi from ever creating a fully Islamist regime inside Sudan, but he did have considerable success for a time in making the country a base and safe haven for all sorts of foreign Islamist groups. Bin Laden's nascent al-Qaeda group was among those that benefited from his hospitality.

Sudan is a very poor country and rather marginal in terms of the politics of the Arab world, so bin Laden's great wealth and growing stature in Islamist circles made him a welcome guest for Turabi and his allies. Repeating his early pattern in Peshawar in the 1980s, bin Laden stayed out of the battle at first. He devoted his time and money for five years in Sudan to recruiting and training al-Qaeda's core membership. While many other Islamist groups carried out terrorist attacks throughout the Arab world and beyond during this period, there is no evidence to suggest that al-Qaeda was a prime mover in any of them. The organization grew in numbers, wealth, skills, and contacts and began to put "sleepers" into place in a number of countries, including Kenya and Tanzania, African countries with significant Muslim populations that were geographically handy to Sudan.

While al-Qaeda gradually put down roots, however, the early 1990s were not a good period for Muslims in general or for Islamist revolutionaries in particular. Any faint hope that a genuinely Islamist government might emerge through the ballot box somewhere in the Arab world seemed totally illusory after the Algerian regime aborted the elections that should have brought the FIS to power there in 1991, and a savage government crackdown in 1992 on the local Islamist movement in Egypt, the biggest and best-organized in the Arab world, seemed to demonstrate the futility of the existing Islamist strategy of local terrorism. Meanwhile, sundry disasters befell small Muslim communities around the world: in Bosnia, in Chechnya, in Kashmir, in Somalia. Most of them were inflicted by non-Muslims, and to bin Laden it all seemed to prove that there was indeed a Satanic Western plot. Western actions to protect Muslims, like the belated NATO military intervention to stop the Serbian massacres of Muslims in Bosnia and even the UN's humanitarian intervention in Somalia, were interpreted by bin Laden as American plots to gain bases in the Muslim lands. It was ideologically unacceptable, and therefore inconceivable, that Christians (as he sees all Westerners) could be moved by a concern for Muslim lives and welfare.

Al-Qaeda's shift from an organizational phase to action may have been precipitated by its expulsion from Sudan in 1996. American and Saudi pressure undoubtedly had a part in this, as did the Sudanese government's eagerness to attract foreign investment to its promising new oil industry, but there is also a widespread view that Turabi, realizing that bin Laden would not take orders and might eventually do something that would get the Sudanese regime into deep trouble, simply decided to move him on. There was by now somewhere else for al-Qaeda to go, for in 1996 the Taliban movement had seized control of most of Afghanistan and effectively brought the civil war to an end except in the far north of the country. Ideologically the Taliban and al-Qaeda were fellow travellers, and bin Laden was something of a hero among Islamist Afghans for his efforts on their behalf during the anti-Soviet war, so the Taliban welcomed him to what was to be his base for the next six years.

Afghanistan was, admittedly, rather far from the heart of the action in the Arab world, where all the other Islamists were still devoting their efforts to trying to overthrow the local regimes. That mattered much less now for bin Laden, however, as somewhere around this time he appears to have made his choice between the "near enemy" (secular regimes in Muslim countries) and the "far enemy" (a.k.a. the Zionist-Crusader conspiracy). Others could devote themselves to trying to overthrow the Egyptian or Saudi regime directly; al-Qaeda would concentrate on attacking the West, and in particular the

United States – in which case it didn't much matter where its base was so long as it was safe. Afghanistan was ideal.

This did not mean that al-Qaeda was abandoning the hope of bringing about Islamist revolutions in Arab countries. On the contrary, it was convinced that the Islamists must gain control of a whole country, and preferably a large one, as a base from which they could proceed to spread their ideas more effectively and expand the area under their control: in practice, this struggle has always been about who controls the Arab states. "Armies achieve victory only when the infantry takes hold of land," wrote bin Laden's senior lieutenant, Ayman al-Zawahiri. "Likewise, the mujahid Islamic movement will not triumph against the world coalition [of Christian and Zionist forces] unless it possesses a base in the heart of the Islamic world." It's just that bin Laden had despaired of getting to this objective by the direct approach, and had decided to go the long way round.

There are very few Middle Eastern experts – and not many politicians or journalists either – who understand that the use of terror for political objectives, like any other human activity that large numbers of people engage in over a long period of time, has developed its own body of theory, strategy, and tactics. The highly ritualized rhetoric usually employed when dealing with the topic tends to phrases like "senseless terrorism," as if people using terror tactics were mad dogs incapable of doing joined-up thinking and having long-term goals. So a little detour into the taxonomy of terror is necessary at this point.

Terrorism is essentially a means of behaviour modification, and it comes in two basic forms: state terrorism and non-state terrorism. State-linked terror, in turn, comes in two common varieties. It is often used by a government against its own people – as in the many police states of the recent past and present where terrorizing the civil population was a normal tool of government – or it may be used against foreign civilians by a government at war.

Terror against foreigners can assume horrendous proportions when it has the resources of an entire industrialized state behind it. During the last four years of the Second World War, for example, British Bomber Command, made up of mostly British and Canadian crews, was destroying civilian lives and property in Germany on a scale equivalent to the World Trade Center losses on half a dozen different nights each month. The American raids on Japanese cities in 1944–45 killed even larger numbers, and the nuclear weapons dropped on Hiroshima and Nagasaki were fifty World Trade Centers at once. Subsequently, the Cold War was all about state terrorism: the United States threatened to drop many thousands of nuclear weapons on innocent Russians if the Soviet government attacked Western vital interests, and Moscow threatened to do the same to Americans if Washington misbehaved in a similar fashion. The death toll, if the Third World War had actually happened, could easily have reached 500 million in a month, more than have been killed in all the other wars of human history, so the "balance of terror" did alter the behaviour of the adversaries quite dramatically.

State-organized terror directed against a country's own citizens can also be an effective behaviour modification device. Stalin's Soviet Union, Hitler's Germany, and Pol Pot's Cambodia are the limiting cases, but Saddam Hussein's Iraq, Ethiopia under Colonel Mengistu, and Argentina under General Videla are pretty good examples too.

Terror carried out by non-state actors is a much less effective technique because their resources are so much smaller. Indeed, the only kind of non-state terrorism with a good record of success is that which occurs in the context of national liberation movements. You are among your own people, so recruiting is easy. The targets are very visible and vulnerable: the foreign occupying forces. And you don't actually have to win the war through terrorism, which is practically impossible. You just have to be enough of a nuisance and a drain on the resources of the occupying imperial or colonial power, and keep going for long enough – and eventually your enemy will decide to cut his losses and go home. That's how the Jewish Underground drove the British out of Palestine in 1945–47, the FLN drove the French out of Algeria in 1956–62, and Frelimo drove the Portuguese out of Mozambique in 1962–75. It is relatively easy for non-state actors in national liberation wars to win through terror, which is why, in the end, men like Archbishop Makarios of Cyprus and Jomo Kenyatta of Kenya both eventually got to have tea with the Queen.

Then there is the weakest form of terrorism: terrorism by non-state organizations against their own governments, or against foreign governments that are not occupying their national territory. This is what the West is up against in its confrontation with al-Qaeda: terrorism at its weakest. From the anarchists who assassinated numerous heads of state in Europe and the United States in the late nineteenth and early twentieth centuries down to the mostly far-left terrorists of the 1960s, 1970s, and 1980s, this sort of terrorism almost never achieves its goals.

One indication of how weak these movements really are is that they almost all follow the strategy best known by the French phrase *la politique du pire*: the strategy of making things worse. Lacking the strength to overthrow the government they hate, the terrorists' strategy is to drive it into an ever more repressive posture by their outrages. If they succeed in making the government ruthlessly oppressive (so the theory goes), then the people at large will finally turn against the government, unite with the "vanguard" terrorists, and rise in righteous wrath to bring the government down. This wish-fulfilment dream of a strategy was first codified in the 1960s by American philosopher Herbert Marcuse, who wrote about the need to "unmask the repressive tolerance of the liberal bourgeoisie," and by the Brazilian terrorist Carlos Marighela, who wrote the *Mini-Manual of the Urban Guerilla* as a how-to guide. This desperately cynical and impoverished idea underlay the strategic thinking (insofar as there was any) of practically every Latin American guerilla/terrorist movement from Argentina's Montoneros in the 1970s to Peru's Sendero Luminoso in the 1990s.

In a more attenuated form, it was also the strategy of the

purely urban "guerillas" who proliferated in the developed countries in the same period. Italy's Red Brigades and Germany's Baader-Meinhof Gang, the Japanese Red Army and the Black Panthers and Weathermen in the United States all believed that their provocations would drive the state into more and more repressive actions that would, in turn, drive the population to support their cause. In reality, of course, while they frequently managed to make the state more repressive – Latin America is full of examples of that – the state then crushed them.

Non-state terror directed against a target that is not a foreign occupier, whether operating within a single state or across the entire international community, has no successes whatever to its credit. Al-Qaeda, to come to our current concern, seems at first glance to be an organization of this last order. Even if it blew up a hundred World Trade Centers or killed a million Americans, it would not bring the U.S. government down or force it to withdraw politically, militarily, and economically from the Muslim-populated parts of the world. And how can terrorist acts against Americans get al-Qaeda any closer to its fundamental goal of bringing Islamist governments to power in major Muslim countries?

Neither Osama bin Laden nor the people around him are stupid: everything about them indicates that they, are intelligent, patient men who plan their actions over a very long term. Could it be that they, too, believe in *la politique du pire* – with the added wrinkle that they hope to provoke the United States into ill-considered actions that will turn the Arab masses against the pro-Western regimes that oppress them and finally get their own long-stalled Islamist revolutions off the ground? The answer, almost certainly, is yes.

It is not clear exactly when al-Qaeda's leaders fixed upon this strategy, though they must have been there at least in a general way by the time they made the "far enemy" their principal target in the mid- to late 1990s. In all likelihood, they arrived at this conclusion by degrees, arguing it through and observing the effects of their earlier actions. Even if they had not fully worked it out in 1998, at the time of their first major terrorist attack, the twin suicide truck-bomb attacks on U.S. embassies in Kenya and Tanzania, President Bill Clinton's response to those attacks would have carried them the rest of the way to their conclusion.

The choice of East Africa for al-Qaeda's first big operation was not surprising, for it had established a number of "sleeper" operatives in Kenya and Tanzania during the years when it was based in Sudan. The choice of American embassies as targets was hardly surprising either. What was unexpected, and very impressive, was that it carried out two attacks simultaneously. This was, as somebody observed at the time, not twice as hard, but a hundred times as hard. Bin Laden, meticulous as always about getting the theology right, issued a fatwa six months beforehand (even though he is not a religious authority entitled under Islamic law to do any such thing) in which he stated, "The ruling to kill the Americans and their allies – civilians and military – is an individual duty for every Muslim who can do it in any country in which it is possible to do it, in order to liberate the al-Aqsa Mosque [in Jerusalem] and the holy mosque [in Mecca] from their grip, and in order for their armies to move out of all the lands of Islam, defeated and unable to threaten any Muslim." Perhaps that was as far as the strategy went at that time – but the twin attacks on August 7, 1998, were a huge success in terms of shock value, killing 224 people and injuring more than 5,000.

The great majority of the victims were Kenyans and Tanzanians (many of them Muslims), sliced to pieces by flying metal in the crowded streets, but twenty-four American citizens were killed in the two embassy compounds. That was the largest loss of American lives in a foreign terrorist attack in a decade, and it posed a major and immediate problem for President Clinton. There was huge pressure on Clinton by the American media, Congress, and the public to punish the guilty parties, and it will be recalled that Clinton had relatively little room for manoeuvre by 1998, as he already had another problem with the American public and media: the little matter of an intern.

The Central Intelligence Agency (CIA) managed to come up with a list of six al-Qaeda training camps in Afghanistan, and added the large al-Shifa pharmaceutical and chemical plant outside Khartoum in Sudan, which it suspected (on rather slender evidence) was making poison gas for bin Laden. In fact, the plant had nothing whatever to do with poison gas – as President George W. Bush's administration finally conceded almost three years later – but Clinton's administration didn't wait for any further verification. On August 20, 1998, two weeks after the embassy attacks, while the UN Security Council was still debating the issue – and only three days after Clinton appeared before the grand jury to answer questions about his relationship with Monica Lewinsky – the United States launched seventy to eighty cruise missiles at the CIA's target list. It was contrary to international law, it didn't do al-Qaeda any serious harm, and it killed lots of innocent people. It was also a public relations disaster – and it may have helped al-Qaeda to finalize the strategy that led to the strikes in September 2001.

The attacks made the U.S. look clumsy, arrogant, and careless of Muslim lives, and there was an outcry in the American media about it, but it did not begin to compare with the outcry in the Arab world. There were double standards at work here, of course – the many Arabs and Muslims who deplored U.S. behaviour on August 20 were a good deal less exercised about al-Qaeda's disregard for African and American lives on August 7 – but legitimate states must expect to be held to higher standards than terrorist organizations. More importantly, the American strikes may have helped to plant the notion among al-Qaeda planners that the United States could be goaded into a massive, indiscriminate attack against targets suspected of being associated with terrorism throughout the Arab and Muslim world if only the initial loss of American lives were great enough.

The best and almost the only publicly available inside account of how al-Qaeda moved from the East African attacks in 1998 to those of September 2001 was given by Ramzi bin al-Shaibah. He had shared a flat in Hamburg with Mohammed Atta and was going to be the twentieth hijacker until he had visa problems getting into the United States; he ended up co-ordinating the operation from Europe instead. In August 2002, he gave an interview in Karachi to Yosri Fouda, a senior journalist with al-Jazeera television, in which he revealed that the preparation for the New York and Washington operations took two and a half years. In other words, the planning began within six months of the East African attacks and Clinton's response, and it is quite likely that it was an attempt to exploit that pattern of events. So focused was al-Qaeda on this huge operation that its sole significant exploit in the interim was the suicide motorboat attack on the U.S. destroyer *Cole* in Aden harbour, Yemen, in 2000 that killed seventeen American sailors.

According to bin al-Shaibah (who was subsequently wounded and captured in Yemen), in early 1999 al-Qaeda's military committee, working in a building known as the House of al-Gumad in the Afghan city of Kandahar, resurrected a previously aborted proposal to fly planes into buildings in the United States and began to refine it. There was a meeting in Kandahar attended by all four prospective pilots before they went off to flight school in the U.S., but the rest of the attack team, most of whom were Saudis, began their training in Afghanistan only in the spring of 2001. They knew it was a "martyr's operation," but did not know precisely what it was until shortly before the hijacks. The original targets apparently included nuclear plants, but the final list included the twin towers of the World Trade Center in New York (code-named

"the faculty of urban planning" in subsequent e-mail communications), the Pentagon ("the faculty of fine arts"), and the
Capitol ("the law faculty"). When he was interviewed in
Pakistan, Ramzi still had Atta's last coded e-mail message from
August 2001 on his laptop computer, detailing the times and
targets of the attacks and the number of hijackers: "The first
term starts in three weeks. . . . There are 19 certificates for
private studies and four exams." Three of the four exams were
successful, and more than three thousand Americans died.

The purpose of the attacks, as Ramzi described it, was "to
cause the greatest possible number of deaths and deal a huge
blow to America on its own soil," and no doubt that is true. But
was that all? Almost certainly not. Al-Qaeda had had almost a
decade to consider its strategy, and it was very clear that the
priority was to find some way of persuading Arab populations
to rebel against their own "apostate" governments, for without
that kind of mass support the Islamist revolutions were never
going to achieve power.

What could possibly stampede large numbers of people who
were not normally willing to risk their lives for the Islamist
cause into coming out into the streets and taking down the
government of Jordan, of Saudi Arabia, of Egypt – of some
Arab country where the Islamist cause could finally gain a territorial base? Well, if you could sucker George W. Bush into
lashing out indiscriminately as Bill Clinton had done, only at
twenty or fifty times the scale (for the offence was certainly
twenty or fifty times as great), then the thousands of deaths of

innocent Muslims that the American counter-strike would cause might just do the trick.

Only George W. Bush didn't walk into the trap. At least, not right away.

CHAPTER III

THE LAW OF MIXED MOTIVES

"What is most important to the history of the world? The Taliban or the collapse of the Soviet empire? Some stirred-up Muslims or the liberation of central Europe and the end of the Cold War?"

– former national security adviser Zbigniew Brzezinski, in 1998

T he answer to Brzezinski's question (opposite) is that it depends where you live. For Brzezinski, who was of Polish descent, it was obviously the liberation of central Europe and the end of the Cold War, although many people would question whether it was really the war in Afghanistan that caused the collapse of the Soviet Union. But it certainly did "stir up the Muslims," as he elegantly put it, and in due course some of them came calling in New York and Washington.

"This isn't going to be a few cruise missiles flying around on television for the world to see that something blew up," said Defense Secretary Donald Rumsfeld a week after the Twin Towers collapsed and his own office was shaken by the plane that hit the Pentagon. He conspicuously failed to hide his contempt for the Clinton administration's violent but incompetent response to al-Qaeda's 1998 attacks on U.S. embassies in Africa, but it's not clear if he considered that al-Qaeda might be trying to elicit the same sort of reflexive American retaliation against an ill-defined target list, but on a far larger scale, with its attacks on September 11. It may have been simply determination to do nothing in the style of the despised Clinton administration that saved the Bush administration from walking into the trap of instant retaliation – or it may be that they actually saw the trap, and walked around it.

Bush's own knowledge of the politics of the Arab world was barely enough to make him dangerous, but he was surrounded by senior advisers who, by sheer fluke, knew a lot. The average senior American politician would have trouble finding the Middle East with a searchlight and both hands, but Vice-President Dick Cheney, Secretary of State Colin Powell, and Defense Secretary Donald Rumsfeld had all served in senior posts in the administration of Bush's father a decade before when he was fighting the Gulf War. They had all visited the region many times, they had met almost all of the Arab leaders, and they had been briefed about the intricacies of Arab politics until their eyeballs were spinning. They were all men who thought in strategic terms, and it is quite likely that once they got past their initial shock and outrage at the attacks they would have asked themselves what al-Qaeda's planners wanted America to do next. The remarkable restraint of the U.S. response – for almost four weeks no American soldier anywhere on the planet fired a shot in anger, and when the counterattack finally began on October 7 it was aimed solely at Afghanistan and carefully restricted to legitimate targets – suggests that they did think the matter through. But if they did, they certainly weren't going to explain their reasoning to the American public.

From the beginning, the Bush administration's public line on the motives for the terrorist attacks has been ultra-simplistic, generally stopping at the assertion that the terrorists are "evil" but occasionally offering the more specific explanation that "they hate our freedoms." This resonates well with a popular mindset in the U.S. that generally assumes, in a semiconscious, quite unexamined way, that nobody else is really free and that everybody else in the world is envious of America, and it is as much of an explanation as most Americans want or need. What imaginable political purpose would be served by trying to educate the American public on the machinations of Islamist forces within the alien world of Arab politics, or alerting them to the rage so many Arabs feel at American foreign policy – and why would you want to hurt people's feelings by telling them that the tragic deaths of thousands of innocent Americans were just an attempt to trick the U.S. government into doing something that would serve the terrorists' agenda back home? If Bush's senior advisers did discern an inner play in al-Qaeda's strategy, they certainly weren't going to share that insight with the American public.

Or maybe they didn't get it at all, and just gave a more serious and methodical response than Clinton's to what was, after all, a much more serious attack. At any rate, they avoided al-Qaeda's trap – and indeed, their responses to this wholly unanticipated crisis between September and December of 2001 were optimal at every level from the tactical to the political. It was a very impressive performance.

The details of the planning and execution of the remarkably successful U.S. military campaign in Afghanistan between October and December can be found in Bob Woodward's *Bush at War*, an uncritical laundry list of a book based on his

privileged access to the major players that essentially recon-
structs the minutes of every National Security Council (NSC)
meeting during that period. What emerges is that the administration very early on defined its primary target as al-Qaeda's
bases in Afghanistan (and the Taliban regime of that country
as well, if it refused to co-operate). It took the task of coali-
tion-building and gaining legal authority for the attack from
the UN Security Council seriously. The Pentagon was encouraged to think creatively about the task of taking Afghanistan,
rather than simply mounting a conventional invasion of the
place, and understood the need to minimize civilian casualties and respect Muslim sensibilities. You really couldn't ask
for more.

There were doubts and hesitations and mistakes, of course,
but it all worked very well. The Russians and the Pakistanis
were amazingly co-operative in providing bases and helping
to persuade the various Central Asian "Stans" to do likewise.
Even the Iranians provided a certain amount of help. The UN
Security Council gave the U.S. a resolution authorizing the use
of force, and most of America's allies agreed to send troops.
The natural reluctance of American generals to invade
Afghanistan, where a long series of previous invaders culmi-
nating in the British and the Soviet armies had come to grief
because of the mountainous terrain, the weather, and the end-
lessly rebellious tribes, was largely overcome by an imaginative
plan to do the job without committing too many vulnerable
American soldiers to ground combat. The idea was to employ
the CIA's agents with local experience, the army's special

forces teams, and suitcases full of cash to mobilize the various anti-Taliban militias across Afghanistan in the service of Washington's campaign, and to pave their way to victory with precision bombing by the U.S. air force. It worked.

Should the United States have attacked a whole country after September 11? In one sense it is an irrelevant question, since President Bush had no real choice in practical political terms: al-Qaeda's strategy had worked at least to the extent that it had put him in a position where he *had* to whack somebody, for American public opinion would have stood for nothing less. Moreover, Bush would have been remiss in his duty to care for American lives if he had not gone after the headquarters from which such a horrendous attack was organized. The Taliban made the decision to take over the entire country of Afghanistan easy for him by obdurately refusing to turn bin Laden and his associates over, which was precisely what the State Department expected them to do, but the United States did go meticulously through the formality of demanding that Mullah Mohammed Omar's ramshackle government in Kabul hand over the suspected terrorists and dismantle al-Qaeda's training camps on its territory. When the Taliban tried to haggle over the terms and it became clear it was not going to comply, Washington went to the further trouble of getting legal authority from the UN Security Council before launching its attack.

Indeed, the generally unilateralist Bush administration was a model of multilateralism (at least in declaratory policy) in the first months after September 11. Washington graciously accepted condolences and offers of aid from dozens of countries, though it ensured that only a few trusted English-speaking allies like the British and the Canadians would have even an honourary place in the order of battle of American forces committed to Afghanistan. The rest were encouraged to contribute to the peacekeeping forces that would be needed in Kabul after the overthrow of the Taliban, since the United States, in Rumsfeld's tirelessly repeated phrase, "doesn't do nation-building." There was a tiny, worrisome hint of things to come in Rumsfeld's insistence in a meeting on September 30 that the United States should not produce a white paper giving the evidence that justified an attack on al-Qaeda – "I think the precedent is bad of having to go out and make your case publicly because we may not have enough information to make our case next time, and it may impair our ability to pre-empt against the threat that may be coming at us" – but for the moment everything was being done with the utmost propriety and even sensitivity.

Even the bombing was being done sensitively, in that the target planners were under explicit instructions to avoid targets likely to cause significant "collateral damage" to civilian lives and property: the White House was well aware that every dead Muslim civilian was grist for al-Qaeda's propaganda mill. One estimate is that during the five weeks of the war, the United States dropped eighteen thousand bombs on Afghanistan, which killed around five thousand civilians. Any ratio lower than one bomb : one dead civilian is evidence for a policy of strict restraint in the choice of targets. The innovative strategy adopted for the attack on Afghanistan, though designed principally to minimize American casualties, also helped to keep Afghan civilian casualties down, for a full-scale ground assault of the traditional kind would have required the use of firepower in a far more extensive and indiscriminate way. All wars kill people, but this one was done with as little loss of life as could be managed.

The genesis of the American strategy in Afghanistan was the decades-long post-Vietnam effort by the U.S. armed forces to devise ways of winning battles with fewer American casualties. One might think this would be a principal focus for all armed forces all the time, and to some extent it is, but generally there comes a point in weapons procurement, just as in automobile construction or highway design, when the level of investment required to reduce the expected death toll among the users any further becomes simply prohibitive. For the American forces after the defeat in Vietnam, however, almost no level of investment was prohibitive if it promised to reduce American deaths in combat, because the lesson of Vietnam was that if American casualties get too high, the public will cease to support the war and *all* of your investment will have been for naught. There was rather more money available in the United States than most governments have to spend, and an efficient lobby to ensure that lots of it went to the military-industrial complex, so the research got done and in due course the new generations of precision-guided and "smart" munitions began to roll out. As recently as the Vietnam War, it was standard practice for an American infantry commander to make an estimate before an attack of how many of his men would be killed and injured in the operation – a cost-benefit analysis, if you like. Now, it is expected that there will be almost no casualties: "smart" firepower will do the work instead.

It was this deliberate and ultimately quite successful attempt to substitute very expensive weapons of unprecedented accuracy and reliability ("one-shot-one-kill" weapons in the vernacular) for the old formula of massed firepower and masses of troops that made possible the extraordinary victories of American-led forces in the NATO interventions in Bosnia and Kosovo in the later 1990s – victories in which not one soldier on the NATO side was killed in combat. Admittedly, these were victories won against a poorly equipped and old-fashioned army more used to massacre than to battle on equal terms, but the Balkan successes, coming on top of the relatively cost-free American victory in the Gulf War of 1990–91 when these new weapons were still in their infancy, led some military experts to talk pompously about a Revolution in Military Affairs (RMA) in which all the old rules had changed and the warrior ethic had been supplanted by mere technological prowess. (Practical soldiers still don't believe this, though they welcome every new weapon that promises to keep their casualties down.) For the American planners in October 2001, the question was how to adapt this new approach to the specific challenge of taking Afghanistan.

It was a more demanding problem than either Bosnia, where the objective had merely been to force the Serbian government to bring its Bosnian Serb proteges to heel, or Kosovo, where the aim was to force the Serbs to end their killing and withdraw their troops from a province whose population was 90 per cent non-Serbian. In Afghanistan, the goal was not only to eradicate al-Qaeda's camps and forces but to destroy and replace the Taliban regime, which implied that there would ultimately be an American military occupation of the country. In the Balkans, the objective had been achieved without using ground troops at all, which was why there had been no NATO combat casualties: it was done entirely by air power, operating in conjunction with friendly local irregular forces. There were numerous potentially friendly militias in Afghanistan too, and so far as possible the U.S. strategy would try once again to combine their efforts on the ground with American arms supplies and air support, in order to avoid the kind of casualties that would be inevitable if American infantry had to be committed to break the Taliban's military resistance. In the end, however, there would have to be what the NSC took to calling American "boots on the ground."

This is not a military history of the brief U.S. campaign in Afghanistan in October-November 2001, but it should be said that it was a triumph for American technology, American special forces, American logistics – and also for American diplomacy. The country was impossibly remote and inaccessible from the sea, only a couple of months remained before the onset of the bitter Afghan winter, and there were fears in the NSC in the month after September 11 that the campaign in Central Asia would stretch far into the next year, while al-Qaeda's leaders remained free to cook up who knew what new and horrible surprises for Americans at home. There were even worries that the Afghan campaign would end up as an American-dominated ground war with lots of American casualties: Afghanistan's reputation for eating up and spitting out invading armies is one of the most deeply entrenched myths of military history. It is a myth because in fact Afghanistan has always been quite easy to conquer: hardly any invading army failed to make it to Kabul. It's just a very hard place to *stay* for very long, because the tribes simply cannot stand having foreigners telling them what to do, and every male over the age of fourteen has a gun. If American troops are still in the country in two or three years' time, what began as a brilliant success may turn into a disaster – but at least it started remarkably well.

While U.S. aircraft carriers sailed towards the Arabian Sea and American diplomats haggled for air bases in the surrounding countries, all of them Muslim, CIA teams began to make their way into the northern one-fifth of Afghanistan's territory still controlled by the losing side in the Afghan civil war of 1989–95, the Northern Alliance. They were unpromising allies for three reasons. One, they were outnumbered two-to-one by the Taliban forces, because they were all drawn from the Tajik, Uzbek, Turkmen, and Hazara minority groups of northern Afghanistan and did not include a single unit from the dominant Pashtun ethnic group. Two, they were divided up into many rival militias that sometimes even fought each other. And three, the Northern Alliance's one widely respected leader, Ahmed Shah Massoud, had been assassinated by an al-Qaeda suicide team posing as television journalists just two days before the September 11 attacks. They were, however, a whole lot more attractive to American planners than the prospect of doing the job with U.S. infantry, so a major effort was mounted to buy them up, arm them properly, and send them against the Taliban and al-Qaeda troops that had faced them for years in largely static trench lines across northern Afghanistan.

The basic concept came from CIA Director George Tenet, who proposed as early as September 13 that the job could be done by CIA paramilitary teams with money to get the various Northern Alliance groups moving and communications equipment to link them up with U.S. forces, to be joined later by military special forces teams that would designate precise targets for massive American air strikes to crush the Taliban troops facing the northerners. It was an easy sale, given the huge drawbacks and delays involved in any other approach, and the first ten-man CIA team, code-named Jawbreaker, arrived in the Panjshir valley in northern Afghanistan on September 26, bearing $3 million in cash and promises of U.S. air support to Gen. Mohammed Fahim, Massoud's successor. American bombs began falling on Afghanistan on October 7, but at first they fell mainly on Taliban and al-Qaeda targets in the south and east because of extensive delays in getting other CIA and special forces teams into position with the various militia groups along the Northern Alliance's eight-hundred-kilometre front line. As time passed with no news except for the daily bombing reports and the impatient U.S. media began to mutter about a "quagmire," the U.S. Joint Chiefs of Staff began to consider the unappetizing possibility of having to send at least fifty-five thousand American ground troops to Afghanistan. At the Pentagon press briefing on November 6, Rumsfeld said he thought it could take months to deal with the Taliban and al-Qaeda. How many months? a journalist asked. "I said months rather than years. That means it could be as long as twenty-three [months]," replied Rumsfeld.

A couple of days later, with half a dozen CIA political teams and a larger number of special forces target designation teams in place at last, massive U.S. bombing cracked open the Taliban positions across northern Afghanistan, and the Northern Alliance began its sweep to victory. Taliban commanders who had already been bribed to change sides kept their promises – the Americans operated on the principle that "You can't buy an Afghan but you can rent one" – and retreat turned into rout. Mazar-i-Sharif, the biggest city in the north, fell on November 9; Kabul was abandoned by the retreating Taliban forces by November 12. When the capital fell the following day, there were just 110 CIA officers and 316 special forces personnel in Afghanistan. By December 7, with the fall of Mullah Omar's headquarters in Kandahar in the southwest, the Taliban regime was no more. It was a remarkable victory.

Desultory fighting continued across Afghanistan for the next several months, as American troops, now present in the country in significant numbers, hunted down the remaining Taliban troops and tried to catch the elusive Osama bin Laden. Some believed he was killed by the huge air strikes called in during the high-altitude battle of Tora Bora in December, but others suspected that he had walked out to safety in Pakistan, and had probably gone to ground in Karachi, a sprawling city of 11 million where he had plenty of sympathizers. Even Mullah Omar got away on his motorbike, leaving a trail of sightings behind him across southern Afghanistan. U.S. diplomats had their hands full coming up with non-Taliban Pashtun leaders to counterbalance the victorious northern ethnic groups who dominated the local scene militarily, in order to have some semblance of ethnic balance in the transitional national government they were trying to create. But these were minor details compared to the fact that the Taliban had fallen and that al-Qaeda had lost all of its bases.

By January 2002, in fact, President Bush was in a position to declare a victory and bring the army home. He could have used the occasion of his State of the Union speech to Congress and the American people in late January to explain that Afghanistan had been the one target in the "war on terror" against which conventional military forces were the appropriate instrument. Most unusually for a terrorist organization, al-Qaeda had had an above-ground base under the open protection of a sovereign state, and so something like a conventional war had been needed to deal with that threat (though mercifully American ground troops did not have to get heavily involved). But, Bush should have explained to his huge audience, terrorists are civilians, and most of the time they live and hide among other civilians, so armies are not normally the right tool to use against them. Police forces and intelligence services and better security measures are what's needed for the long haul in the war against terror, not bombers and soldiers.

He could have said, Go home, folks, the show's over. The war on terror is now moving into a second, much longer phase in which, most of the time, it's going to be all but invisible. We'll be working our fingers to the bone to track down the remaining al-Qaeda members and their associates, but most of the time you won't hear anything about it – not even when we're successful. U.S. forces will have to stay in Afghanistan for a little while, until we get a new, democratic Afghan government up and running properly, but then they'll be coming home, and I don't anticipate that we'll be making big military commitments elsewhere in the near future. It just isn't that kind of war. Thank you, God bless America, and good night.

He could have said that. He should have said that. But he didn't. Instead, he told a startled world that he had discovered the "axis of evil."

It was a Monty Python moment. For four months the only topic had been al-Qaeda, Osama bin Laden, Islamist terrorism . . . and all of a sudden it was "Now For Something Completely Different." Iraq, Iran, and North Korea – three regimes that had almost nothing in common and barely spoke to one another – had suddenly been lumped together as a joint menace to human civilization, and the United States was going to tame or remove their regimes one at a time, starting with Iraq. It was the turning point of the post–September 11 world: before the "axis of evil," the cascade of events, however surprising, made an ugly kind of sense; afterwards, it made a great deal less.

Bush got a relatively easy ride in the mainstream American media, where the post–September 11 chill on comments that breach the new rules on patriotism and solidarity inhibited criticism of the great war leader, but elsewhere people simply didn't know where to look. "All European nations would view a broadening [of the war on terrorism] to include Iraq highly skeptically," said Germany's foreign minister, Joschka Fischer, in a December 2001 *Financial Times* interview. "We know which nations' representatives and citizens were fighting alongside the Taliban and where their activities were financed from. Iraq is not on this list," said Russian President Vladimir Putin a few months later. Canada's foreign minister, Bill Graham, normally the soul of discretion when discussing American policies, could not understand what the Bush administration was up to: "Nobody is supporting Saddam Hussein, but everyone recognizes in international politics you have to have a process where, before you invade a sovereign country, there has to be a reason for it, or we are going to have international chaos." Even ultra-loyal Britain's foreign secretary, Jack Straw, was at a loss to explain it all, and suggested to British reporters that it was not so much a new American strategy as a vote-winning device "best understood by the fact that there are midterm congressional elections coming up in November." (Condoleezza Rice, Bush's national security adviser, replied coldly, "This is not about American politics, and I assume that when the British government speaks about foreign policy, it's not about British politics." There was not another squeak out of Straw.)

But how did it actually happen? How did Iraq, a secular country whose dictator, Saddam Hussein, was himself a target for al-Qaeda's hatred, end up on a list alongside Iran, a country with which Iraq had fought a bitter eight-year war quite recently, and whose ruling Shia theocracy was equally abominated by the Sunni fanatics of al-Qaeda? And how did North Korea, the world's last Stalinist dictatorship, a non-Muslim country separated from the other two by all of Asia, end up on the same list? What did they have in common, apart from the fact that none of them had anything to do with the terrorist attacks on America? For that matter, why were Syria and Libya, which have backed international terrorists (though not al-Qaeda) much more recently, left out of the axis of evil?

It was all so bizarre that the satirists had a field day. "Diplomats from Syria denied they were jealous over being excluded," wrote Andrew Marlatt in a fake news report posted on SatireWire.com less than a week after Bush's speech, "although they conceded they did ask if they could join the Axis of Evil. 'They told us it was full,' said Syrian President Bashar al-Assad. 'An Axis can't have more than three countries,' explained Iraqi President Saddam Hussein. 'This is not my rule, it's tradition. In World War II you had Germany, Italy, and Japan in the evil Axis. So you can only have three. And a secret handshake. Ours is wicked cool.'" Marlatt went on to detail the frantic geopolitical realignments as everybody else raced to set up their own little club of three: "Libya, China, and Syria . . . formed the 'Axis of Just As Evil,' which they said would be way eviler than that stupid Iran-Iraq-North Korea axis. . . .

Cuba, Sudan, and Serbia said they had formed the Axis of Somewhat Evil, forcing Somalia to join with Uganda and Myanmar in the Axis of Occasionally Evil . . . [while] Canada, Mexico, and Australia formed the Axis of Nations That Are Actually Quite Nice but Secretly Have Nasty Thoughts About America." All good fun, but one year on the process that was launched by that foolish phrase is about to culminate in a major war in the Middle East, and tens of thousands, or quite possibly hundreds of thousands, of people may die. Why did the subject suddenly change just over a year ago?

The question of including Iraq in America's post–September 11 target list came up in the first National Security Council meeting after the attacks, on September 12, raised by the attack dogs of the administration, Donald Rumsfeld and Paul Wolfowitz. The "unfinished business" of 1991, when concern about American casualties had stopped the first Bush administration from sending American troops to Baghdad to get Saddam Hussein, had continued to engage the attention of subsequent administrations, and at Rumsfeld's direction the Pentagon had been working to develop a viable military option for an attack on Iraq. But Osama bin Laden was no more likely to have an alliance with Saddam Hussein than he was, say, with Kim Jong Il, and even Rumsfeld was merely proposing, in effect, that Iraq be smuggled into the attack program while American public opinion was still willing to support almost any military action directed against Arabs. Secretary of State Colin Powell opposed the idea because it would immensely complicate his task of building a coalition for the Afghanistan operation, and Bush put an end to the discussion by saying that his goal was to go after the terrorists. Soon after, however, former CIA director James Woolsey was tasked with searching for any evidence that might link Saddam Hussein to al-Qaeda. Already on record as advocating the overthrow of Saddam Hussein, he gave it his best shot, but came up empty-handed after months of digging.

Rumsfeld and/or Wolfowitz returned to the subject of attacking Iraq in at least three subsequent meetings of the NSC in September, according to Bob Woodward's account, and presumably didn't abandon the topic afterwards either. Their obsession with Iraq became widely known in Washington outside White House circles, and was attributed by some to their close links with Israel, for an American attack on Iraq was more obviously desirable from an Israeli point of view than it was in terms of America's own interests. But nobody else on the NSC went along with their ideas – not even famously hard-line Vice-President Dick Cheney, who observed, "If we go after Saddam Hussein, we lose our rightful place as good guy" – and most professional U.S. army officers thought it was a dreadful idea. It is striking, however, that almost all the senior Republicans in the administration (which did not include CIA Director George Tenet, a Democratic appointee) took it for granted that Iraq should become a target eventually. Their disagreements were just about timing and tactics: even despite the total lack of evidence implicating Saddam Hussein in al-Qaeda's actions and the inherent improbability of such an alliance, they believed that he must somehow be involved – as if everybody who has a quarrel with America is automatically in the same gang. Bush himself summed it up in his closing remarks at the NSC meeting of September 17: "I believe Iraq was involved, but I'm not going to strike them now. I don't have the evidence at this point."

He never would have the evidence, but four months later he began to move against Iraq anyway. The first that White House speech writer David Frum heard about it was in late December when his boss, chief speech writer Michael Gerson, came to him and said, "Here's an assignment. Can you sum up in a sentence or two our best case for going after Iraq?" The essence of the task was to find some way of linking Iraq and al-Qaeda at least rhetorically, in the absence of any evidence of real links between them. Frum found himself turning to Franklin D. Roosevelt's speeches in the days after the Pearl Harbor attack in December 1941, for Roosevelt had faced a rather similar problem: he believed that Germany posed the greater threat to long-term American security, but it was only Japan that had actually attacked the United States. Hitler had solved Roosevelt's problem for him by declaring war on the United States in support of his Japanese ally on December 11, 1941, but Saddam Hussein was not going to oblige George W. Bush in the same way, so Americans had to be talked into having a war with him. Frum came up with the phrase "axis of hatred" to evoke the shadowy links between Iraq and al-Qaeda that he wanted to make Americans believe in, and Gerson tweaked the phrase into "axis of evil" to make it sound more "theological." National Security Adviser Condoleezza Rice, impressed by the anti-regime street demonstrations that had broken out in Tehran at the time, then suggested adding Iran to the list in the belief that it would help the demonstrators along, and somebody else – it's not clear who – tacked on North Korea to ensure that the list was not all Muslim countries and to bring it up to the magic number of three. (Andrew Marlatt was right.) Thus is policy made and the world reshaped.

Frum, one of those right-wing Canadians who thrive in the more congenial ideological environment of early twenty-first-century America, was thrilled by the speech when Bush addressed Congress on January 29, 2002. "I thought it was one of the great moments of American history," he gushed in a *Guardian* interview. "I thought it was magnificent. Even though I know I shouldn't be surprised by Bush, I am always surprised. Up until the last, he looks like he might compromise and do the small thing. And then he does the big thing." Alas, Frum's equally gushy wife, Danielle Crittenden, e-mailed all her friends saying, "I realize this is very 'Washington' of me to mention, but my husband is responsible for the 'Axis of Evil' segment of Tuesday's State of the Union address," with the almost inevitable result that her boast leaked to *Slate* on-line magazine and soon afterwards David Frum lost his job. Still, what Bush did *was* a "big thing." In effect, he issued postdated declarations of war on three sovereign countries.

In two cases out of three, of course, he didn't really mean it: that's just what happens when you let speech writers make foreign policy. By mid-2002, the phrase "axis of evil" had been excised from the administration's vocabulary, and it's no wonder. Iran has three times Iraq's population and a relatively homogeneous and united population that showed recently (in the war with Iraq) that it will fight back ferociously against an invader. Besides, its government is far from being a pure dictatorship: the Khomeinist mullahs still control the courts and the police, but there is a parallel, freely elected government that competes with them for power. Even if the United States has no present intention of attacking Iran, however, a U.S. occupation of Iraq would immensely complicate relations with Tehran. "As the occupying power, we will be responsible for the territorial integrity of the Iraqi state," observed Charles William Maynes of the Washington-based Eurasia Foundation in September 2002. "That means we will have to move our troops to the border with Iran. At that point Iran becomes our permanent enemy."

North Korea has a regime with no redeeming features whatever, but it certainly has enough fissile material for a couple of nuclear bombs and it may even have the weapons. It also has the fourth-largest army in the world, and even a conventional war in the Korean peninsula would cause a totally unacceptable number of casualties. The crisis began with Bush's inclusion of North Korea in his "axis of evil" speech, which frightened Kim Jong Il out of his wits, but Washington has no intention of attacking an almost-nuclear power. In the end, the diplomats will almost certainly be allowed to make a deal. But Iraq, on the other hand, that's something U.S. forces could actually do.

Whether it is desirable to do it is another matter, but it's clear that George W. Bush thinks it is. The real questions, to paraphrase the old Watergate formula, are what does he want (in Iraq), and when did he want it? The answers are not simple ones, however, because the Law of Mixed Motives always applies.

The law just states the obvious – that all motives are always mixed – but it's remarkable how many people find mixed motives intolerable and insist on a single, fixed one as the explanation for an event, particularly for a large event. For example, the recent revelation (by Bob Woodward of the *Washington Post*) that President Bush ordered the U.S. military to update its plans for the invasion of Iraq only six days after the September 11 attacks will be taken by some people as proof that this is what he intended from the start. Indeed, the extreme conspiracy theorists will claim it as "evidence" that the U.S. and/or Israel staged the terrorist attacks on New York or Washington themselves, in order to give themselves an excuse to overthrow Saddam and seize Iraq's oil.

What it really means, in all probability, is just that Bush was trying to cover all the bases. In the chaotic early days after the attacks in New York and Washington, before Bush had a clear idea of who had been involved in planning and backing the attack, it would have been mere common sense to set a number of military planning processes in motion on a contingency basis, and his personal background as much as the instincts of his colleagues on the NSC would have inclined him to give Iraq pride of place on the list. Nor should we assume that the military took this to mean any more than "update the plan in case we need it": as part of the centuries-old general staff process, they habitually maintain plans for the invasion of practically everywhere. There's no "smoking gun" here. There's not going to be one anywhere. So, what does he want, and when did he want it?

A constant in the behaviour of the Bush administration since September 11 has been an absolutely fanatical determination not to allow another attack like that to occur in the United States. That would be a rational goal and indeed a high priority for any administration, but in the Bush White House it goes well beyond that: eliminating even the slightest chance of such an event has become the overriding priority, to the point where all other measures of national interest are eclipsed and all negative side effects are ignored. The citizens of New York City would no doubt applaud this single-minded concentration on the goal, but the result is not necessarily sensible.

A rational calculation of the likelihood that Saddam Hussein will get a nuclear weapon in the next five years would yield a probability of well under 10 per cent, given that he was already under a strict embargo and would remain under some form of strict international supervision until the day he dies no matter how the UN sanctions were eventually refashioned. Let us be deeply pessimistic and calculate that there is a one-in-five chance that if he got such a weapon, which he has dedicated decades and billions to acquiring, he would give it to some faceless terrorist who would then try to smuggle it into

America. (One can't readily imagine *why* he would do that, but never mind.) That gives us an overall probability of under 2 per cent that leaving Iraq uninvaded in 2003 will result in somebody trying to smuggle a nuclear weapon into the United States before 2008. Now try to calculate the odds that invading Iraq in 2003 will trigger other changes in the region that are a bigger threat to American security – like an Islamist coup in Jordan, leading to a new Arab-Israeli war and another catastrophic Arab defeat that radicalizes millions more throughout the Arab world, or an anti-American coup in Pakistan, which already has lots of nuclear weapons and could spare a few for terrorists. You can't really come up with reliable numbers for this sort of thing, but nobody who knows the region would put the likelihood of such an upheaval in the wake of a U.S.-Iraq war at less than 10 per cent. So it doesn't make sense to attack Iraq in terms of enhancing American security if you consider all the likely side effects and long-term repercussions – but at the moment all of that is being subordinated in practice to the obsession with eliminating any perceived immediate threat, however minuscule. "Not again on my watch" is the ruling mentality, and to that extent al-Qaeda has succeeded in hijacking American foreign policy after all. There has been another hijacking as well, however, and this one was an inside job.

Back in 1997, during the Clinton administration, Donald Rumsfeld, Dick Cheney (then-CEO of Haliburton, the world's biggest oil-field services company), and a group of other neo-conservative Republicans, most of them also involved in the oil business, created a lobby group called Project for the New American Century, which advocated "regime change" in Iraq. In 1998, they sent letters calling for Saddam Hussein's removal to President Clinton, the Senate majority house leader, Trent Lott, and the speaker of the house of representatives, Newt Gingrich. Among the signatories of one or more of the letters, in addition to Rumsfeld and Cheney, were Paul Wolfowitz, now Rumsfeld's deputy at the Pentagon, John Bolton, now undersecretary of state for arms control, former CIA director James Woolsey, and Richard Perle (a.k.a. "The Prince of Darkness"), currently chairman of the Pentagon's Defense Policy Board. Another notable signatory was Zalmay Khalilzad, who was a consultant to Unocal Corporation when it was seeking to build a pipeline across Taliban-ruled Afghanistan (a project stopped by the Clinton administration), later served as Bush's special envoy to Afghanistan in the winter of 2001–2002, and was appointed by Bush as a special official for Iraq in January 2003. The letter to Gingrich – five years ago – stated that "we should establish and maintain a strong military presence in the region, and be prepared to use that force to protect our vital interests in the Gulf – and, if necessary, to help remove Saddam from power." To what extent might these views be connected with the fact that the Middle East contains 70 per cent of the world's known oil reserves, a proportion that is bound to rise over time since other oil-producing areas are depleting their reserves at a much faster rate?

"Ninety cents a barrel for oil that sells for $30 – that's the
kind of business anyone would want to be in. A 97 per
cent profit margin – you can live with that."

> – John Teeling, CEO of the Dublin-based
> oil company Petrel, currently exploring
> a concession in Iraq, November 2002

Well, of course! many people would say. It's all about oil. "Our
oil is the main reason America wants to attack Iraq," says Ali
al-Rawi, head of the economics department at Baghdad
University. "They want to control our oil and control price
and production levels. They know the future oil resources for
the world will continue to come from this area for many
years." Considering that the United States must already
import half of the 20 million barrels it consumes each day,
and that high oil prices cut into the economy's growth rate, it
all seems quite obvious. Iraq has the second-largest oil
reserves in the world, but it's only pumping about a million
barrels a day because of UN sanctions against Saddam's
regime and the rundown state of the oil fields after a decade
with hardly any new investment. Get rid of Saddam, rebuild
Iraq's oil infrastructure, and the country could be pumping
6 million barrels a day within five years – three-quarters as
much as Saudi Arabia normally produces. An American-
controlled Iraq would give the United States a kind of insurance policy against an Islamist revolution in Saudi Arabia
(which alert Americans were already worried about in the late
1990s, well before they learned that fifteen of the nineteen

hijackers on September 11 were Saudis). As a bonus, it would also give the U.S. the ability to break the power of the Organization of Petroleum Exporting Countries (OPEC) by flooding the market with Iraqi oil, thus guaranteeing long-term low prices for America's favourite commodity. *Of course* there's a conspiracy; *of course* it's about oil. I think we've solved this one, Watson. Next case.

But hang on a minute. Why would a bunch of senior people in the American oil industry – none of these men was in government in 1998 – want low oil prices? American consumers do, and sometimes politicians try to fulfill their desires, but why would American oilmen want to take over Iraq and push its production to the limit in order to cut the price of every barrel of oil they sell from there and everywhere else? Especially since many of them also have interests in new oil-field developments in North America, where the relatively high cost of production means that the fields are only worth developing if the world market price is high. It doesn't really make a lot of sense when you think about it – and neither does the argument about taking over Iraq as insurance against an Islamist revolution in Saudi Arabia, where the United States currently buys about 15 per cent of its imported oil. Hidden in there is the unexamined and patently silly assumption that oil-producing countries will only sell their oil to their friends, or perhaps only to those who actually control them. This misconception underlies a great deal of debate about the strategic importance of this or that oil-exporting country, as if they were doing you a favour by selling it to you. They are not.

If Monaco happened to be sitting on the world's richest oil field, then possibly it could afford to take its time about developing it and choose its customers with care. It's already rich, and it doesn't need the cash flow. Not one of OPEC's members fits that description, however, nor do any of the major non-OPEC producers like Russia and Mexico. They have people to feed and care for and educate, so they must sell their oil to pay for the food and services they need. There is a unified global market for that oil, with a single price for any given grade from any given region on any given day, and you sell it to whomever wants to buy it. When the Ayatollah Khomeini came back to Tehran in triumph in 1979 and turned his country into the Islamic Republic of Iran, the usual panic-mongers worried about Iran cutting off oil exports to the West, but in fact Iran has pumped every barrel it could within OPEC quotas (and sometimes beyond them) in every year since then. Great Satan or not, the U.S. – anybody, in fact – can buy its oil. Iran had 35 million people to feed even then, and didn't produce enough food to meet the demand itself; now it has 65 million people, and around half the meat they eat comes from Australia and New Zealand. Where else will the money to pay for it come from, if not from oil?

The same applies to Saudi Arabia, the current focus of concern. Back in 1973–74, when it led the one and only Arab oil embargo against the developed world, the Saudi kingdom had fewer than 8 million citizens. Now it has 22 million, and they cannot live by drinking oil. It must be sold not just to keep them in comfort, but literally to keep them from starvation, and

Saudi Arabia could no more withhold its oil from the market for six months than its major customers could live off their strategic oil reserves for that long. Even Osama bin Laden, if he ruled Arabia (it certainly wouldn't be called "Saudi" Arabia any more after the Saudi ruling family was deposed), could not stop exporting oil for long. Indeed, during January 2003, while Bush orated almost daily about the need to attack Iraq, the United States was buying up about half of Iraq's monthly output of oil to top up its strategic reservoirs in the salt caverns on the Gulf of Mexico in anticipation of the coming war – and Saddam Hussein was happy to sell it. It's called the free market, and it works very well.

The argument about oil prices, by the way, is equally hollow. The Saudi Arabians have argued for decades that the price of oil must remain in a middle band (currently between $20 and $30 a barrel), in order to maintain a decent income without destroying OPEC's ability to act as a cartel at all. OPEC members start to starve at around $10 a barrel, since oil is generally their main source of income, so they must not flood the market with so much oil that they make the price drop that low – and by the way, it's entirely up to them to manage the overall level of global supply, since all the non-OPEC countries are usually producing oil at full capacity. (It's not all fun being a cartel.) That is why the OPEC oil ministers meet every quarter to set production quotas for each member. Produce too much, and you just hurt yourself.

Get too greedy and produce so little that oil prices soar, on the other hand, and you also hurt yourself. When oil prices rise to more than $30 a barrel, it becomes economically viable for Western oil companies to start developing alternative sources of oil in non-OPEC parts of the world, where the production costs per barrel are generally far higher than they are in the ultra-cheap Middle East, including the more exotic options of offshore oil in deep water and the immense reserves (bigger than Saudi Arabia's) locked into the tar sands of Alberta. After a few years, non-OPEC oil production soars, OPEC's market share drops, and its members are worse off than if they had never started the game. At that point, the OPEC countries drop their production curbs and pump more oil, the oil price drops – and the whole cycle starts again. Thus OPEC went from a 55 per cent share of global production in 1973 (with very low oil prices) to a mere 30 per cent share in 1986 (though with very high prices, relatively speaking), and has since clawed its way back up to its current 42 per cent share (which is still barely enough to let it operate as a price-fixing cartel). Nobody wants to go around that cycle again: eventually OPEC learned that everybody, both producers and consumers, gets hurt badly at some point in the cycle if the price oscillations become too extreme. So the name of the game now is to damp the swings down, and the country with prime responsibility for doing that is Saudi Arabia, because it is the swing producer in OPEC, the only one with such large reserves and such enormous production capacity that it can go from producing 6 million barrels a day to 10 million (or back again) in a couple of months. This makes Saudi Arabia the natural "enforcer" in OPEC: if the other, economically desperate members get too ambitious on the price front, it can just raise its production, flood the market, and bring the price tumbling back down. It does it too.

Does Riyadh play this role because the ruling Saud family (seven thousand princes at last count, but the true number may be twice that) are American puppets? Not at all. Some of their short-term fine-tuning of the oil price may be done to help their American patrons, but their main motive is to preserve the long-term value of their truly immense reserves. If oil prices ever rose to $50 a barrel and stayed there, it would be a matter of a very few years before the main customers in the industrial world restructured their economies to substitute alternative energy sources for oil wherever possible, thus dropping total demand for oil, and the price it can command, back down toward the lower end of the range. In fact, if you push the customers too hard on price, they may change their pattern of energy use radically and irreversibly, in which case those huge reserves of oil you are sitting on, which you thought would look after not just the grandchildren but the great-grandchildren, will turn out to be fairy gold. There just won't be a market for it – ever.

There is nothing arcane about all this: anybody with a basic understanding of market economics should get it instantly. If you are the only sandal-maker in town and you decide to start charging $100 per pair, how long will it be before somebody else sets up in the sandal business and charges only $75 – and somebody else starts cutting up old rubber tires and selling the tread as sandals at $35 a pair? When Osama bin Laden talks about how a post-Saudi, Islamist Arabia should sell its oil for $144 a barrel, he's just spouting nonsense: he comes from a business background, and knows perfectly well that Arabia would have to go on selling its oil at world market price. There is no alternative market to the industrial and industrializing countries of Europe, the Americas, and Asia; the producers can't afford to stop selling the oil to them or their people starve – and they can't even fiddle with the price very much. But if the idea that you must control your suppliers in order to secure your oil supplies is a mercantilist illusion left over from the eighteenth century, then why do seemingly intelligent American politicians and businessmen go on and on about the need to protect or control oil-producing regions of "vital national interest"? Why has the United States, for example, spent decades supporting regimes like those in Saudi Arabia and Algeria?

The whole notion that the customers must control the suppliers in order to assure constant supplies had a tiny bit of truth during the Cold War, because the east-west struggle was usually a zero-sum game. Every country where the American-backed regime lost control tended to become a Soviet client, and then Moscow might be able to cut off the flow of oil from there in a crisis. But the old Soviet Union is a dozen years gone and the zero-sum game is over: if the United States loses influence in some Middle Eastern capital now, no global strategic rival takes its place. But it is still perfectly possible that some *commercial* rival of your oil company might get its government to back it in a questionable deal with the host country that freezes you out, so it's still handy to have your own government on side to apply some leverage in your favour. It happens in other commodity trades too, but it happens far more in the oil world because people tend to think in familiar old grooves, so it's easy to persuade politicians and the general public that supporting an American company, for example, in some tricky negotiation in a foreign country is in the national interest and not just that particular company's commercial interest. Even if what's really driving the show is corporate profits and executive stock options, oil deals very often get discussed in a "strategic" context.

What is true for oil companies is doubly true for Israel, which must keep the United States convinced of the strategic importance of Middle Eastern oil if it is to maintain the unlimited U.S. military commitment to Israel that most Israelis see as crucial to their survival. For they remember, even if most Americans don't, that the United States was not always allied to Israel: in the Suez-Sinai War of 1956, for example, when Israel conspired with Britain and France to attack Egypt and seize the Suez Canal, it was the United States that forced them to stop and give it back. Only when Egypt and Syria became full-fledged Soviet clients after that war did America become Israel's closest ally in the region, and at that point it made perfectly good strategic sense for both countries. Israel was in confrontation with Arab countries that were backed and armed by America's enemy, the Soviet Union, so their interests ran in parallel. But that old strategic rationale vanished with the Soviet Union in 1991, and American support for Israel now rests mostly on a foundation of habit and sentiment. Israeli governments, fearing that that might not be enough in the long run, therefore put a huge effort into cultivating friends in the American political system who can help to persuade the U.S. government that the two countries really still do share common strategic interests after all. In practice, that means persuading official Washington that Israel's most dangerous enemies in the Middle East – Saddam Hussein's Iraq, obviously, but also Saudi Arabia – are also America's enemies.

This is a perfectly legitimate enterprise of diplomatic persuasion of the sort that all governments, including the U.S. government, frequently engage in. It is America's job to sort out its own strategic priorities, and if a foreign government manages to persuade many members of its élite that they have a common security problem, then fair enough. The only reason Israel's operations of this sort in the United States become controversial is because – again quite rationally – it sometimes attempts to stifle an analysis of those operations by suggesting that the critics are anti-Semitic. That is how *Nation* magazine got into such hot water in September 2002 for pointing out how many members of the Bush administration had close connections with pro-Israeli lobby groups: Vice-President Dick Cheney, Undersecretary of State for Arms Control John Bolton, and Undersecretary of Defense for Policy Douglas Feith (number three at the Pentagon) all served on the advisory board of the Jewish Institute for National Security Affairs before taking up their current jobs, and Defense Policy Board chair Richard Perle and former CIA director James Woolsey are still advisers. There's nothing illegitimate about it, but it does suggest that these people will share Israel's views on its enemies in the Middle East.

This was very likely the genesis of the remarkable briefing delivered to the Defense Policy Board in September 2002, when Perle invited Rand Corporation analyst Laurent Murawiec to make a presentation to the board that painted Saudi Arabia as "the kernel of evil, the prime mover, the most dangerous opponent [of the U.S., which] supports our enemies and attacks our allies." The administration had to distance itself from the presentation after it leaked out that Murawiec had advocated blowing up Saudi oil fields and damaging the country's financial assets unless it assisted more actively in the struggle against terrorism.

It is less clear whether it explains the creation of a "B team" within the Pentagon to come up with evidence justifying an attack on Iraq, for many of the top people around Bush, including Rumsfeld, Wolfowitz, and Perle, also belong to a loose group of neo-conservative defence intellectuals who have been seeing mortal threats to American security behind every tree since the late 1970s. Some of them took part in the original B team exercise under President Gerald Ford, which was an alternative intelligence operation with the task of second-guessing CIA estimates of Soviet defence spending in order to justify higher U.S. defence spending. (The B team claimed, naturally, that the Soviet military budget was much higher than the CIA estimates, but in fact even the CIA estimates, based on a grossly inflated calculation of the size of the Soviet economy, were too high.) Late in 2001, Rumsfeld set up another B team at the Pentagon headed by Douglas Feith, with the task of finding some evidence – any evidence – that would allow him to dispute the CIA's conclusion that there were no links between al-Qaeda and Saddam Hussein.

This is where the stories come from that Iraq has fissionable material, anthrax and botulism toxin, even smallpox, and that it is harbouring senior members of al-Qaeda. Former CIA agent Robert Baer, who investigated al-Qaeda while serving with the agency, explains that the data the Pentagon team is using comes from defectors eager to prove their value to the U.S. intelligence services in order to merit special treatment on green cards, resettlement expenses, and the like – people "who come out of Iraq and tell one horror story after another. But the information gets so polluted by the time it gets to the CIA that they've been turning them away. So the neo-conservatives are processing this information to make a more favourable case against Iraq. It isn't new – they did it to Gaddafi. Cooking the intelligence is a tried and true way to get your will in Washington."

Bush also carries some personal baggage. Many people suspect there is an element of family vendetta in his Iraq fixation – Saddam Hussein allegedly plotted to assassinate Bush's father during a 1993 visit to Kuwait, and Bush is certainly planning Saddam's death now. Maureen Dowd pointed out in a hilarious column in the *New York Times* in August 2002 that there may also be an Oedipal rivalry at work: Bush cuts taxes because his father raised them, and takes Baghdad because his father didn't. ("What we need here is family therapy," she concluded.) In his book *The Right Man*, the first tell-all insider account of the Bush White House, David Frum, for all his manifest admiration of the president, talks about how the beliefs and attitudes of evangelical Christianity shape this little society: Bush has come to believe that he was "chosen" to lead, and that September 11 "revealed" what he had been put in the White House for. And there's no question that Bush positively thrives on being a war leader: he's gaining new gravitas by the month, and may soon sprout Churchillian jowls. All of which may be profoundly relevant to the administration's targeting of Iraq, or utterly irrelevant, but it probably goes into the mix somewhere.

A desperate desire not to be surprised again, oil industry manipulation, Israeli strategic priorities, Bush family ties – all of these considerations are background data in a way: attitudes, experiences, lobbies, and personalities that predispose the Bush administration to concentrate on certain foreign enemies, real and imaginary, rather than others, and in general to hyperventilate on security issues. None of it specifically explains why the Bush administration decided to nominate Iraq as lead player in the axis of evil in January 2002, or why the United States is seriously planning to invade Iraq in 2003. And we should at least be open to the possibility that these are two separate questions. Assume an administration obsessed with covering every risk, and suffused with an abiding suspicion of Iraq quite regardless of the evidence available: we still have to explain why Iraq made its way to the top of the list in January 2002. Could the answer have anything to do with the fact that the war in Afghanistan ended in December 2001?

George W. Bush was not a very popular president before September 11, 2001: about 40 per cent of the American population believed he had stolen the presidency with the help of his brother, the Republican governor of Florida, and the Republican appointees on the Supreme Court, and his "job approval" rating in the last opinion poll before September 11 was only 55 per cent. Then came the attacks on the World Trade Center and the Pentagon, and Americans closed ranks behind their commander-in-chief: by early October, patriotism and solidarity in a time of crisis had driven his job approval rating up to an absolutely unprecedented 90 per cent. At that point, on October 7, Karl Rove, who in effect is Bush's domestic political manager, produced a two-page analysis of the latest polling data that remarked upon the huge surge in the president's popularity, "unparalleled in modern polling," but warned that "the durability of such increases is usually only seven to ten months." It had happened exactly that way to Bush's father during the Gulf War of 1990–91: he had an approval rating of 59 per cent before Saddam Hussein invaded Kuwait, soared to 82 per cent at the height of the crisis, and was back down at 59 per cent nine months after the war ended. Throw in a recession, and he managed to lose the election just nineteen months after his victory in the Gulf. Rove took this data to President Bush and told him that if history was any guide, they could expect only thirty to forty weeks before the opinion polls returned to normal. "Don't waste my time with it," said Bush, as decorum obliged him to say in the middle of a war – but he did look at the numbers.

Fast forward three months to January 2002. Bush's ratings have held up remarkably well during the autumn as events unfolded in Afghanistan, but now the war there is over and Osama bin Laden is either dead or on the run. By Rove's calculations, Bush's ratings are due to sink back to normal just in time for the midterm Congressional elections in November, when the Republicans desperately want to win back control of the Senate – and there's a recession on that could seriously damage the administration, and news of the Enron scandal is starting to break. What a pity that we had to win the war just now. It would certainly help if we could keep some sort of war going at least until November. Not a real war with people getting killed, you understand, but a sufficiently convincing prospect of a real war later on to keep Bush's ratings high and distract attention from these other awkward issues.

It may have worked like that, though everybody involved would be obliged to deny it loudly and indignantly in public (and perhaps even to themselves). There was a slapdash "round up the usual suspects" sloppiness to the way they came up with the notion of an axis of evil that does suggest it was driven more by political than strategic motives. Indeed neither the military nor the intelligence services were involved in any way in the birth of the concept. The one thing that the nominated countries had in common, apart from non-involvement in terrorist attacks against Americans, was that they were all familiar hate figures to the American public for reasons long predating September 11: Iraq because it was still run by the Gulf War enemy, Iran because it had humiliated America after its revolution a quarter-century ago, and North Korea for reasons going back half a century to the Korean War. Tell the nervous American public, which knows very little about "abroad," that they are all ganging up together against the United States now, and you'll make an easy sale.

Was it really that cynical? It would certainly not be unique in the annals of politics if it were, and besides, you have to remember that the United States didn't actually declare war on anybody in January 2002. The administration just laid out a menu of new enemies to worry about, and discuss future wars against, in order to keep the public busy and interested. It is even likely that in the minds of those peddling this vision it was a two-way bet at the time: we'll talk about a war with Iraq until November, and once we're safely past the election we'll decide whether we really mean to do it. In the meantime it's just talk, and we can always walk away from it later if it turns out to be a bad idea.

Maybe that's how the attack on Iraq originally got on the agenda, but once you start a wagon like this rolling down the track, lots of other people start to pile their baggage on board too. Big Defense industry and Big Oil, both with strong ties to the administration, saw all sorts of opportunities in a war with Iraq, and the right-wing lobby in Washington that views American global hegemony as the only source of American

security started to come up with sweeping ideas for refashion-
ing the entire Middle East in America's image, and the media
and Bush's allies abroad started picking away at the idea, which
forced him to defend it and committed him a little more
deeply than perhaps he originally intended, and all the while
the wagon was picking up speed. Soon, the basic position of
the administration had mutated into "anybody who hates the
United States and seeks weapons of mass destruction will have
to be destroyed," a preposterous and quite infeasible policy
entirely at odds with fifty years of the policy of deterrence –
but by now, deterrence was out and pre-emption was in. And
since the new policy is indefensible in international law if
stated too baldly, it had to be softened for international public
consumption by fabricating links between the regimes that
America is going to target and the terrorists who might actually attack it. Already in March 2002, Vice-President Cheney
was claiming to the press, "We know that [Saddam's regime]
. . . would use such weapons should they be able to acquire
them. We have to be concerned about the potential marriage
between a terrorist organization like al-Qaeda and those who
hold or who are proliferating knowledge about weapons of
mass destruction." To people who know nothing about the
politics of the region, it sounded plausible enough.

By spring, administration spokespersons were regularly
talking about the need for "regime change" in Iraq (a phrase
first used in the Project for a New American Century letter to
President Clinton in 1998), which implies a U.S. invasion of the
country and at least a transitional military occupation, but

there was little urgency about it. No matter how much speed the bandwagon was picking up, nobody in the administration had the slightest intention of going to war until the November elections were safely past: war fever can be helpful electorally, but body bags are not. At the end of August 2002, when the political season reopened and the first anniversary of September 11 drew close, suddenly there was endless talk of war from administration sources, and the long-delayed debate was joined – on patriotic ground where the Republicans could not lose. Issues like the recession and the Enron scandal, which would normally have served the Democrats well, were largely obscured in the media by the intense focus on the question of war with Iraq. Bush's numbers held up well through the whole year, and Rove's strategy (if such it was) worked brilliantly; in November the Republicans duly triumphed in both houses of Congress. So it was time for the Bush administration to revisit that two-way bet and consider whether it really wanted to go ahead and attack Iraq. Only it turned out that the decision had taken itself in the meantime: the momentum was too great to stop it.

It's not just a question of Bush having painted himself into a corner with his tongue, though by now it would be very difficult for him to walk away from his warnings about Iraq without acting on them. The matter has got into the courts, so to speak, in the sense that in early September Bush was persuaded by U.S. Secretary of State Colin Powell and British Prime Minister Tony Blair to take the matter of Iraq's alleged weapons of mass destruction to the UN Security Council, rather than just attacking the place unilaterally with a so-called "coalition of the willing" (i.e., the U.S., Britain, a few other NATO members, and the Australians). Powell's and Blair's aim was to ensure that if the United States did declare war, at least it would have some legal cover, and they stood a very good chance of getting it. Hardly any other government thought that an invasion of Iraq was actually a good idea (including most of those who would send troops to Iraq if Washington did attack), but there was still room for a deal because everybody on the Security Council understood that the United States could not be declared an international outlaw no matter what it did.

The entire philosophy behind the UN Charter is that you gradually tame the great powers and seduce them into accepting the rule of international law by giving them the leading role in the proceedings and (at least for the first generation or two) a veto that grants them immunity from having to submit to the law themselves. In the very long run, if you're lucky, they will realize that the universal enforcement of international law is in their own general interest, even if it occasionally clashes with their particular interests, and finally you will have an international system genuinely based on law, not on power. But we are still a very long way from the promised land, and in practice the UN takes an ultra-realistic view of how the great powers behave.

If the greatest power of all decides to do something the other major powers think is a bad idea, but not one that will actually bring the roof down, then they are not going to wreck the whole organization in an attempt to stop it. They will try to talk the superpower down, tie it up in endless negotiations, and generally Gulliverize it, but in the end if it insists on continuing, they won't die in a ditch over it. Most of them won't send troops or help in any other way, but they will give the superpower some sort of fudged legal cover and wait for better times, because the alternative of destroying the UN is much worse.

It was largely in this spirit that the UN Security Council, after almost two months of haggling, passed Resolution 1441, which sent UN arms inspectors back into Iraq in November 2002. The inspectors had been withdrawn, largely at American insistence, in 1998, after a long and messy history of systematic obstruction by the Iraqi authorities and systematic recruitment of the inspectors as spies by both the United States and Israel. Despite all that, Iraq's nuclear weapons program had been comprehensively dismantled and the great bulk of its chemical and biological weapons destroyed during the eight years the inspectors were active, and regular American and British bombing sorties over the four years since the inspectors had been withdrawn helped to curb any Iraqi attempts to revive those programs. Nobody thought that Saddam Hussein was meticulously complying with the provisions of the 1991 agreement in which he had promised to get rid of all his nuclear, biological, and chemical weapons and longer-range missiles in a verifiable manner, but on balance most governments believed the situation was under control: Saddam was effectively contained, and the sacrifices and risks involved in forcing him to observe every last letter of the agreement would be more trouble than they were worth. But President Bush thought differently – in January 2003, he told the press, "After September 11, the doctrine of containment just doesn't hold any water as far as I am concerned" – and that fact would have to be accommodated.

So the UN Security Council decided to send the inspectors back to Iraq and gave the United States a resolution that didn't exactly say that it could attack Iraq without getting permission from the council if the inspectors failed to find what Washington said was there, but didn't exactly say that it couldn't attack unilaterally either. It cost the U.S. nothing to go through the UN because it was not ready to attack Iraq at an early date, anyway: major U.S. troop movements to the Middle East didn't really start until the Congressional election was out of the way.

Is there any way that the Bush administration could have been diverted from its goal of attacking Iraq? It's certainly not inconceivable: another terrorist attack on American territory that refocused popular attention on al-Qaeda, or the capture or death of bin Laden, could shift American attention from Iraq overnight. But I write this assuming that the war will happen. How bad might it get?

CHAPTER IV

HOW BAD COULD IT GET?

"All of us are saying: 'Hey, United States, we don't think this is a very good idea.'"

– King Abdullah II of Jordan, July 2002

"I always kid him and say, 'Mr President, there is a reason why your father stopped and didn't go to Baghdad. He didn't want to stay for five years.'"

– Senator Joseph Biden, then chairman of the Senate Foreign Relations Committee, July 2002

The most striking thing about the Bush administration's approach to an invasion of Iraq is that it has behaved throughout as if the actual military job of conquering Iraq would not pose any kind of problem. It dawdled through the first eight months of 2002, doing nothing much in the way of military buildup or diplomatic preparation in the region although it had already designated Iraq as the prime menace to American security, then went into rhetorical high gear in the two-month run-up to the November elections, but only began moving troops into the region in a large way in late November-early December. Then all of a sudden in January 2003 it became a matter of the utmost urgency to attack Iraq almost at once, even if it meant pulling the UN arms inspectors out with their job less than half-done. It's easy enough to explain all this in terms of American domestic concerns – the need to spin the crisis out until the midterm elections, the desire not to frighten voters with call-ups of reserves and the like until the votes are actually cast, and then the resultant pressing timetable if the campaign is to be fought before the arrival of the hot weather in Iraq in April makes everything much more difficult – but it betrays a great insouciance about the ability of the Iraqis to do anything about America's intentions. The civilians in charge of the Department of Defense – the so-called "chickenhawks" like Donald Rumsfeld and Paul Wolfowitz – seem genuinely convinced that the Iraqi people will rise up and get Saddam within days of the start of the attack, after which resistance will collapse. In that case they don't really have to worry much about the actual military conduct of the war beyond the first overwhelming strikes – and they don't appear to.

They could be right, which is why the low-end estimates of a special UN task force set up to forecast the extent of the humanitarian crisis in Iraq after a war are only 7,200 civilian dead and 3,200 soldiers. The high-end estimates, on the other hand, are 86,000 Iraqi civilian deaths and 80,000 military deaths, plus another half-million people needing medical treatment and 3.6 million made homeless (out of a population of 26 million). The huge difference between the lower and upper estimates is almost entirely due to the fact that nobody really knows if the Iraqi army, or at least a large part of it, will actually fight against the invasion. The people around Bush are pretty sure that it won't – that the first set of images out of Iraq will be American tanks crossing the Tigris bridges surrounded by cheering throngs, and the second set will be "strange fruit" hanging from the lampposts as the population takes its revenge against the members of Saddam's Ba'ath Party – but not everybody else is so confident. If the Iraqi army resists, the images will be very different.

There's not much point in asking serving American soldiers what they think about all this, since military discipline prevents them from giving you a frank answer. There was a spate of leaks to the *New York Times* and the *Washington Post* last July of various competing plans for the invasion of Iraq, some perhaps orchestrated by the administration but others quite probably coming from officers who did not like or trust the plans they had been ordered to make, and wanted them exposed to public ridicule in order to be rid of them. If so, those officers have now been hunted down and silenced, for there has not been a single indiscretion from the U.S. military in recent months. Yet you can still learn a good deal about their views if you pay close attention, and the first thing you realize is that the civilians are almost always a lot more optimistic than the soldiers. "The first Gulf War was fought like the Second World War, with air dominance – pounding their defences, softening up the forces, and then going in," says Daniel Gouré, a military analyst at the Lexington Institute in Washington. "This will be speedier, more precise – an effects-based operation. It will be much more surgical, both in the use of explosive force and in the overall operation." Yes indeed, says John Pike, director of GlobalSecurity.org, another Washington think-tank, who predicts that the military operation will last little more than a week: "I think when this war is written up, it will emerge as the re-emergence of the importance of land power." They have all these neat new toys, from Stryker fighting vehicles to microwave bombs, and they'll just run rings around any poor Iraqi soldiers who try to resist.

The people who actually have to do it, the professional soldiers, are more cautious; like farmers, they have learned that there's a lot of the environment you can't control. Their reflexive pessimism is as much a professional deformation as the boyish enthusiasm of the civilian defence experts, so you have to apply some windage the other way – but it's still noteworthy how unconvinced they are about the wisdom of their superiors. Listen to former Marine Corps commandant Gen. James Jones, now in command of U.S. forces in Europe, in December 2002, taking issue in the *Washington Post* "with those who seem to think this is pre-ordained to be a very easy military operation," or retired Gen. Norman Schwarzkopf, U.S. commander during the 1991 Gulf War, worrying aloud in a January 2003 interview with the same newspaper about how Donald Rumsfeld doesn't listen to professional advice: "When he makes his comments, it appears that he disregards the army. . . . And before I can just stand up and say, 'Beyond a shadow of a doubt, we need to invade Iraq,' I guess I would like to have better information." British military officers have been more outspoken: Gen. Sir Michael Rose, former head of the SAS and of UN forces in Bosnia, warned, "There are huge political and military risks associated with launching large-scale ground forces into Iraq," and Field Marshal Lord Bramall, a former chief of defence staff, recently predicted that an invasion of Iraq would pour "petrol rather than water" on the flames and provide al-Qaeda with more recruits. He also quoted a predecessor who said, during the British invasion of Egypt in the 1956 Suez crisis: "Of course we can get to Cairo but what I want to know is what the bloody hell do we do when we get there?" as if the same question might apply to Baghdad.

Old soldiers out of touch with the new technology, perhaps – but hundreds of young American soldiers have been pushed through the U.S. army's urban warfare training facility in Fort Polk, Louisiana, every day since November. Somebody in charge thinks there might be street-fighting in Iraq after all. (The mock-up of a town where they practice their craft is called Shughart Gordon, by the way, after two of the nineteen American soldiers who lost their lives in one day's street-fighting in Mogadishu in 1993 – which is seriously indiscreet, given what happened to American public opinion shortly after that.) Maybe the young Americans will not need the skills they learn at Shughart Gordon in Iraq, but if they do, the whole high-speed, low-cost victory assumed by the White House and the Pentagon technocrats goes down the tubes, and everybody is back in the harsh old world of hard choices and big losses. It all depends on the answer to a single question: Will the Iraqi army and people fight for Saddam Hussein, or welcome the American invaders with open arms?

Donald Rumsfeld regularly makes a childish analogy between Saddam Hussein and Adolf Hitler – "Think of all the countries [in the late 1930s] that said, 'Well, we don't have enough evidence.' I mean, *Mein Kampf* had been written, Hitler had indicated what he intended to do. Maybe he won't attack us. Maybe he won't do this or that. Well, there were millions of people dead because of the miscalculation." If this analogy were true, then of course the Iraqis would fight to the end for Saddam. The Germans went on fighting for Hitler months after the war had obviously been lost. They even went on fighting in the ruins of Berlin after 95 per cent of the Reich had been occupied, losing five poorly trained teenagers for every Russian they managed to kill in a desperate street-by-street battle to defend the Führer in his bunker under the Reichskanzlerei for just one more day. If Saddam Hussein is the new Hitler, then the U.S. army is in deep trouble. But of course he isn't: Iraqis don't love him that much, and he isn't very powerful.

Hitler became the dictator and idol of 80 million Germans in the centre of Europe at a time when Germany was the world's second- or third-largest industrial power and even America and Russia had populations of under 150 million. In only twelve years of furious activity he conquered almost all of Europe, had 6 million Jews and other "undesirables" murdered in death camps, was driven back from his conquests in a war that cost tens of millions of lives, and committed suicide in his bunker. At almost sixty years' remove, it still impresses and appalls.

Saddam Hussein, by contrast, rules over a country that ranks about fortieth in the world by Gross Domestic Product (about the same as Connecticut), in an area of great oil wealth but practically no heavy industry or high technology. He has been at or near the centre of power in Iraq for thirty-five years, and in absolute control for the past twenty-three years, and during that time his secret police and army have killed several hundred thousand of his own people – bad even by Middle

Eastern standards, though the Syrian, Iranian, and Sudanese governments over the same period of time come fairly close. He has also waged two wars against his neighbours, but they were not part of some master plan for the conquest of the Middle East. On the contrary, they grew out of territorial disputes between Iraq and its Iranian and Kuwaiti neighbours that long predated Saddam Hussein's birth, and out of contemporary political events like the Islamic revolution in Iran in 1978 that sought to extend its influence to the oppressed Shia majority among Iraq's population. He even managed to lose both of those wars, and Iraq is not a millimetre larger today than it was when he came to power. As the new Hitler, he just doesn't make it. Even if he were the first-born son of Satan, he lacks the power base to be truly dangerous to anybody outside his immediate neighbourhood.

Calling somebody Hitler pushes the right buttons among the historically challenged majority, and it also lets you portray yourself as the new Winston Churchill in a "titanic struggle of good and evil" (as Bush put it in several speeches last year), so it will remain a popular game. The truth, however, is that both Churchill and Hitler are long dead, and this is about a sixty-five-year-old Iraqi man with a smaller paunch than Churchill's and a bushier, greyer moustache than Hitler's. He has been in power so long because he is the most ruthless player of the political game in a country that all Arabs acknowledge to be the toughest to rule in the whole region: it is a country that has always been held together, and held down, by force. He has never been an Islamist fanatic, or even noticeably devout. He is no longer a socialist ideologue, though he once was (and built a quite impressive welfare state in Iraq in the days before the wars when the oil revenues were flowing freely – he even encouraged Iraqi women to become the most emancipated in the whole Arab world). He is not anti-American by conviction, though nobody in the Bush administration seems able to understand that. On the contrary, he thought he had a firm if unofficial alliance with the United States after the war with Iran, and utterly miscalculated America's response to his annexation of Kuwait in 1990 because he knew little about the world outside Iraq. In his famous conversation with U.S. Ambassador April Glaspie in the summer of 1990, Saddam thought he was getting American clearance to invade Kuwait when he spoke to her about Iraq's territorial claim to the country and she replied that the U.S. had "no opinion." Glaspie, on the other hand, had no idea that Saddam could be so ignorant as to imagine he could get away with a straight-forward cross-border invasion, took his remarks as purely hypothetical, and went off on holiday. That blunder, rather than some fiendish master plan, is how he fell into the desperate situation he has been in for the past dozen years. Now he's just trying to stay alive, and perhaps pass power on to one of his sons – and he knows that no Iraqi leader in the past half-century has left power alive except for the one he overthrew in 1979, his cousin and mentor Ahmed Hassan al-Bakr. He is tough, clever, and desperate, and the question that must preoccupy him as much as it does the U.S. army is whether the Iraqis will fight to defend him.

They did in the war against Iran in 1980–88, fighting against three-to-one odds in conditions as bad as those on the old Western Front of the First World War – and sticking it out for twice as long as the Europeans without mutinying (as the French, Russians, and Italians did in 1917 after only three years of trench warfare). *And* they stuck it out even though more than half the soldiers in the trenches were Shias, co-religionists of the Iranians and a politically underprivileged majority in Iraq, where the Sunni minority of the central region have always kept the key positions of power for themselves. On the other hand, most of Saddam's troops did not fight with any enthusiasm against the American-led coalition in the Gulf War in 1991 (not that they had any real chance to fight, stuck out there in the desert and helpless under the crushing air superiority of the allies). After Iraq's defeat in the Gulf War, both the Kurds and Shias revolted against Saddam's rule – but the Sunni Arabs stayed with him, and put the rebellions down. Nobody knows which way the various communities will jump this time.

The domination of Iraq by the Sunni Arabs, only a quarter of the population, is not an invention of Saddam. It dates back to Ottoman times, when the Turkish rulers of the region preferred to recruit their local troops and administrators from the Sunni Arabs who lived around and north of Baghdad because they were not rebellious, like the Kurds farther north, and were of the same orthodox Sunni faith as the Turks themselves, unlike the Shia Arabs south of Baghdad. It was not a country in those days, of course, just the three Ottoman vilayets (provinces) of Mosul, Baghdad, and Basra, but when the British empire moved in after the First World War and put them together as Iraq (complete with puppet king and army), they found it perfectly natural to perpetuate the preference for Sunni Arabs when recruiting local collaborators. Most of the British had served in India, where co-opting local minorities was standard operating practice. The Sunni Arab dominance persisted into the independence period, given their deeply entrenched position in the army, government, and business, and indeed persists to this day. Saddam Hussein is a Sunni Arab himself, born in the town of Tikrit north of Baghdad, and over the decades of his power has ensured that most of the key posts around him and throughout the army remain in the hands of Sunni Arabs. The most sensitive ones are often held by his own clansmen from Tikrit, tied to him by blood loyalty, but many other men are bound equally firmly to him by what has been called "a coalition of guilt" – so deeply implicated in corruption and in the regime's many atrocities that they know they must sink or swim with Saddam.

So who will defend him and who will defect? The Kurds – 20 per cent of Iraq's population but a non-Arab people with close relatives in adjacent parts of Turkey, Iran, and Syria – are already mostly beyond his control, living in the autonomous areas in the north created under the protection of coalition air power after 1991. They were not all loyal to Baghdad even in the Iran-Iraq War of the 1980s, and would accept at most an arm's-length relationship even with a post-Saddam regime in Baghdad. The Shia Arabs of the south, who make up close to 60 per cent of the total population, stayed loyal during the

Iranian war (maybe because the Ba'athist regime had raised their living standards dramatically in the previous decade), but turned on Saddam after the Gulf War of 1990–91 and joined the Kurds in a rebellion that almost destroyed both the regime and the country. Critics of President George Bush senior's refusal at the time to back those revolts and thereby finish Saddam Hussein off avoid the point that if the revolts had succeeded, the country would probably have split in three, with a new Kurdish republic in the north seeking to liberate its brothers in Turkey and Iran, a Shia Islamic republic in the south that would ally itself with Iran and scare the Gulf Arabs half to death, and a rump Sunni Arab state around Baghdad with a very big chip on its shoulder. But that didn't happen because the Sunni Arabs did not abandon Saddam in 1991 even in defeat. They fought for him methodically and effectively, first reconquering the whole of the Shia south amidst vast and indiscriminate bloodshed, and then retaking at least the lowland areas of Kurdistan where the northern oil fields are. They may not love Saddam – indeed, many of them have lost a relative in his prisons or his wars – but they know that his fate and the fate of Sunni Arab rule in Iraq are now inextricably intertwined. If he goes down, so do they, in the most profound historical sense, so they may fight for him again. And they are the people the U.S. army would have to go through to get at Saddam in his bunker in central Baghdad.

So if the CIA doesn't have a deal with somebody who has access to Saddam to kill him on the first day (CIA Director George Tenet has estimated the chances of that at no more than 15 per cent), what would the second Gulf War look like? The Iraqis have had no navy and virtually no air force since 1991, and this time nine out of ten American bombs will be "smart" (as opposed to one out of ten last time), so in the first couple of days it would look like a high-tech cakewalk. American aircraft using second- and third-generation "smart bombs" would destroy Saddam's palaces, military command and control centres, electricity-generating installations, and all the other facilities the Iraqis would need to conduct a co-ordinated defence of the country if that were their intention – and American and British ground forces coming in from Kuwait and possibly Turkey and Jordan would effortlessly slice through whatever troops Saddam Hussein leaves as a screen on the frontiers and race towards Baghdad and the other major cities. The only imponderables are whether American airborne troops could secure all of the widely scattered oil fields before Saddam's people blow them as they did the Kuwaiti oil fields in 1991, and whether Basra, the great city of the south and an almost entirely Shia town, surrenders without a fight to the Marines who storm ashore at Fao. If Saddam still has any Scud missiles left in the western desert towards Jordan, within range of Israel, this is also when he would take them out of hiding and fire them, before he loses them. It would be surprising if even fifty American soldiers died in this phase of the operation, though of course many thousands of Iraqis would die. But then American troops would arrive at the outskirts of Baghdad, Tikrit, and the other cities of central Iraq, and we would all find out if the Sunni Arab part of his army is going to fight for Saddam or abandon him.

The Iraqi army has 375,000 soldiers, deliberately slimmed down by half from the unwieldy force of Gulf War days, and Saddam Hussein will keep the best troops away from the frontiers and the open desert where they can easily be destroyed by American air power. They will be in the cities, and above all in Baghdad, positioned where they can put down any anti-Saddam revolts easily and hoping to draw American troops into close-quarters street-fighting where U.S. air superiority and smart bombs are not so useful. The 50,000 to 70,000 men of the Republican Guard, a well-trained, almost entirely Sunni Arab force whose soldiers stood by their posts and fought in 1991, will form the outer ring of defences in the urban areas, while central Baghdad will be held by the 26,000 troops of the ultra-loyal Special Republican Guard, 80 per cent of whose officers come from Saddam's home region of Tikrit. "If I were [Saddam]," said Dennis Gormley, a consulting senior fellow at the International Institute for Strategic Studies, "I would be telling the Republican Guard to bed down in urban areas, near shrines, hospitals – anywhere collateral damage might be a concern. They have the ability to deliver chemical weapons at short range. Street-fighting would severely limit the technological superiority of U.S. and British troops, and if they are forced to don chemical garb, it would reduce their effectiveness by 30 to 40 per cent." Even then the Iraqi goal would be not to win – that's not possible – but just to hang on, force the U.S. to use heavy weaponry in built-up areas and kill lots of civilians, and inflict enough casualties on U.S. troops to make the U.S. public have second thoughts about the war. Even if ten Iraqi troops died for every American soldier killed (and the ratio could be much worse than that for the Iraqis), a few days of street-fighting could take the U.S. forces up to the Mogadishu line – or so Saddam hopes. It's a slim hope, for no matter how many American casualties there are, it's still unlikely that American public opinion would have time to turn around on the war before Saddam is dead in his bunker, but what other strategy does he have available?

We can be reasonably sure that this will be Saddam's strategy because it's the one he adopted in 1991 in case the Americans kept coming after the liberation of Kuwait, and because no other strategy makes any sense in his predicament. But we should bear in mind that another part of his 1991 strategy was to try to draw Israel into the war by firing missiles at Israeli cities. If Israel could be lured into retaliating with missile strikes against Iraq, it wouldn't make Saddam's life much harder – once the U.S. air force is on your case, the rest is details – but it would drastically change the optics of the conflict in Arab eyes. It would no longer be an American-Iraqi war, but a war in which the United States *and Israel* were attacking an Arab country together. The fury in the streets throughout the Arab world would be so intense that no Arab government could go on supporting the American action even tacitly, and several would be at risk of overthrow. It didn't work in 1991, because Washington persuaded Jerusalem not to

retaliate even though Iraq fired thirty-nine Scud missiles at
Israel. But that was a different Israeli government. This one
says that it will retaliate.

Why would Prime Minister Ariel Sharon's government fire
back this time, even though it knows the wave of violence
that action would unleash against American interests and
America's allies throughout the Arab world? Perhaps because
Israel has its own fish to fry. There is a delusion in the Arab
world (one shared by many Americans) that American and
Israeli interests and strategies are identical, but of course
they are not. Israel is a separate country in a quite different
part of the world, with its own priorities and its own internal
disagreements. Sometimes its goals are very different from
Washington's, though it always strives to keep the differences
hidden from ordinary Americans, and this may be one of
those times.

The key fault line in the Zionist movement, even fifty years
ago, was the division between those who were willing to share
Palestine with its Arab inhabitants, and those who insisted
that everything west of the Jordan River must be theirs. The
split first surfaced in 1947, when the World Zionist Congress
voted to accept the United Nations resolution partitioning the
Palestine mandate between Jews and Arabs – and 160 "revisionist" delegates rejected the proposal. Their contemporary
descendants populate today's governing Likud Party, whose
central committee voted last May to reject statehood for
Palestinians under any circumstances, and although Sharon

actually opposed that resolution for tactical and diplomatic reasons, he has always been a leading light of the revisionist camp in Israeli politics.

The problem for all of Israel's revisionists, until recently, was that a majority of Israelis *did* want to exchange territory for peace. Sharon's brutally direct solution to that problem, after the failure of the Camp David summit in July 2000 gave him a window of opportunity, was to march onto the Haram al-Sharif/Temple Mount in Jerusalem that September surrounded by almost a thousand troops and police. His purpose, many Israelis suspected at the time, was to provoke a Palestinian uprising that would end peace talks and bring down then-prime minister Ehud Barak. That was the result, at any rate, and once Sharon became prime minister in early 2001, he not only failed to suppress the intifada, but behaved in ways that had the seemingly counter-productive result of stoking it. "Targeted assassinations" of Palestinian resistance leaders were often carried out just when moderate Palestinians were trying to persuade the groups sending out the suicide-bombers to stop the attacks, at least against civilians living within the legal borders of Israel as laid down in the 1948 armistice, and indiscriminate repression of the general Palestinian population helped to keep the temperature high. Maybe it was just incompetence, but perhaps it was a strategy aimed at changing Israeli attitudes.

In 2000, less than 8 per cent of Jewish Israelis favoured the drastic and illegal measure called "transfer": the expulsion of all 2 million Palestinians from their homes in the West Bank and their forcible "transfer" across the river to Jordan. Most people thought it was an impossible and immoral proposal. By August 2002, two years and a hundred suicide-bombers later, a Tel Aviv University survey found that 46 per cent of Israeli Jews backed "transfer." Indeed, 31 per cent of Israeli Jews even supported the expulsion of their Arab fellow citizens, who comprise one-fifth of all Israelis. If that is the desired consequence of a deliberate policy, as the left-wing press in Israel frequently alleges, then what was Sharon's purpose in manipulating events in order to shift Israeli opinion in this way? Martin van Creveld, Israel's most respected military historian, thinks it is to prepare the way for wholesale ethnic cleansing of the West Bank.

In an article in Britain's *Daily Telegraph* newspaper in April 2002, van Creveld wrote: "Mr Sharon would have to wait for a suitable opportunity, such as an American offensive against Iraq . . . [or] an uprising in Jordan, followed by the collapse of King Abdullah's regime . . . [or] a spectacular act of terrorism inside Israel that killed hundreds. Should such circumstances arise, then Israel would mobilize with lightning speed. . . . A force of 12 divisions, 11 of them armoured . . . would be deployed: five against Egypt, three against Syria, and one opposite Lebanon. This would leave three to face east [against the West Bank and Jordan] as well as enough forces to put a tank inside every Arab-Israeli village just in case their populations get any funny ideas.

"The expulsion of the Palestinians would require only a few brigades. They would not drag people out of their houses but use heavy artillery to drive them out; the damage caused to

Jenin would look like a pinprick by comparison. . . . Some believe that the international community will not permit such an ethnic cleansing. I would not count on it. . . . America will not necessarily object . . . particularly if it does not disrupt the flow of oil for too long. Israeli military experts estimate that such a war could be over in just eight days. If the Arab states do not intervene, it will end with the Palestinians expelled and Jordan in ruins. If they do intervene, the result will be the same, with the main Arab armies destroyed. Israel would, of course, take some casualties . . . [but] their number would be limited. . . ."

Is this what Sharon secretly intends? It is impossible to know, and he would certainly deny it in public, but if the United States invades Iraq, we could learn the answer quite quickly. All that can be said in the meantime is that Sharon has always argued that Israel's only hope of safety lies in its own strength, because Arabs can never be trusted, and that he has opposed every proposal to return conquered territory to the Arabs from the peace deal with Egypt down to the Oslo accords.

What if van Creveld's fears turn out to be right? Then Jordan would really become the Palestinian state that Israeli revisionists have always said it should be, a seething nest of misery whose embittered inhabitants blame everybody else, non-Arab and Arab alike, for the disasters that have befallen the Palestinian people. The rest of the Arab world would face a decade of terrorism and revolutionary upheavals. Israel would be quite a lot bigger, at least for a while, but it would have forfeited any prospect of a peace settlement with its Arab neighbours for at least a generation – by which time the balance of forces in the Middle East, currently so favourable to Israel, might have shifted dramatically against it. Nobody can guarantee that the Arab states will always be poor and disunited, that Israel will always have a nuclear monopoly in the region, and that the United States will forever be Israel's closest ally and the dominant power in the region: Israel needs to make peace with its neighbours and have a few decades for everybody to get used to the idea before any of the current circumstances shift. "Transfer," if it happened, would not just be a moral outrage and another terrible blow to the Palestinian people. It would also be a long-term disaster for Israel, but disasters sometimes do happen.

"The big worry for everyone, including me, is what would replace [Saddam]. Nobody – nobody – would accept the installation of a government by a foreign power. America seems to think that Iraq is somehow like Afghanistan, and it isn't."
– Baghdad businessman, November 2002

Whether the Iraqis fight to defend Saddam Hussein's regime or not, and regardless of whether Israel is drawn into the war or not, it is very likely that Saddam will be dead and American troops will control the centre of Baghdad within a fairly short time after the bombing starts: "weeks, not months," as Bush likes to say. With luck, Saddam's forces will not have used chemical or biological weapons in their fight, thus averting the nuclear response that both the United States and Israel say they might resort to in that case. A great many Iraqis will be dead, of course, but the state of the surrounding countries will largely depend on whether the casualty toll is ten thousand or hundreds of thousands, and on how Israel behaved during the war. If there is little fighting and a low casualty toll, and Israel stays out of the war, the immediate damage to the status quo elsewhere in the Middle East may be little more than some badly shaken regimes and a number of U.S. embassies burned to the ground. If there is a lot of fighting in Iraq, huge Iraqi civilian casualties, and large-scale participation by Israel – rocketing Baghdad, invading southern Lebanon, clearing Palestinians off the West Bank – then the region may be hard to recognize by the end. The most vulnerable regimes are those in the immediate vicinity of Iraq and Israel that are politically tied to the U.S. – Jordan, Saudi Arabia, and Egypt – but pro-American governments as far away as Algeria could go down before the wrath of the mobs or the anger of nationalist junior officers. There is also the question of Pakistan, the only non-Arab Muslim country where Islamists are a very influential group (mainly because the confrontation with India continually emphasizes the Islamic component of the country's identity). The current ruler, Gen. Pervez Musharraf, has defied popular sentiment by co-operating with the U.S. in the war in Afghanistan. An American invasion of Iraq could trigger a coup by Islamist officers in the Pakistani army – and Pakistan, of course, has nuclear weapons.

The beneficiaries of these revolutions, if they occur, would be local Islamist groups in almost every case – probably not al-Qaeda members as such, but like-minded people who would be happy to extend the same hospitality to bin Laden's organization that it once enjoyed in remote Afghanistan. The United States, if it follows its own logic, would then be obliged to invade those newly revolutionary countries as well . . . but let us be charitable and assume there will not be this kind of domino effect. Let's assume, in fact, that every existing regime in the region, however decrepit and corrupt, survives the crisis with the sole exception of Saddam Hussein's. Then all that the United States would have to contend with, apart from a major rise in support for al-Qaeda, is the military occupation of Iraq (and the continuing occupation of Afghanistan, of course, for Mohammed Karzai's regime there would not survive a month without American protection). How hard can that be?

It could be very hard. Iraq is a notoriously difficult country even for native-born rulers to govern, because it is made up of three major and quite self-conscious populations – Kurdish, Sunni Arab, and Shia Arab – that have neither a common language nor religious tradition, nor even a consensus on such basic values as pan-Arab nationalism. One of the reasons Iraq has such a long history of oppressive and brutal rulers is because gentler ones would not succeed. For a foreign country to take on the responsibility of governing Iraq, precisely at the point where a long-established oppressive regime has been destroyed and every group senses that this is the moment to push hard for its own communal goals, would make for an interesting time.

The plans for the occupation regime are taking shape, revolving around an American military governor on the model of Gen. Douglas MacArthur in Japan after the surrender in 1945 (probably Gen. Tommy Franks, the current head of Central Command, which has the prime responsibility for the campaign in Iraq). He would be assisted by a UN-approved civilian administrator – various people who have already done similar jobs in the Balkans (like former French health minister Bernard Kouchner, American diplomat Jacques Klein, and former U.S. ambassador to Indonesia Robert Gelbard) have been mooted for the role – and the cabinet minister, deputy minister, and provincial governor-level posts now filled by Ba'athist officials would all be taken over by U.S. military officers. The various exiled Iraqi opposition groups would essentially be frozen out, and the U.S. would run the entire country for up to two years (paying its expenses out of Iraq's oil earnings) while preparing free elections to choose a democratic Iraqi government. However, since none of America's regional allies would countenance the breakup of Iraq, it must be a "democratic decision" that confirms the country's unity – which could mean finding a (not entirely democratic) way to put the Sunni Arab minority, who are committed to a unified Iraq, back in the saddle. "The Americans will have to handle security Iraq-wide for quite a while with peacekeeping help from the usual suspects – the European countries and Canada," predicts David Malone, head of the International Peace Academy, a New York–based think-tank. "But the civilian management of Iraq is something they may not want to take on."

It could all work out in an orderly and reasonable manner, but it's at least equally probable that there will be violent chaos in the country, with various groups taking revenge on each other and everybody hunting down the Ba'athists who have ruled the place so cruelly for so long. The Kurds in the north will be hoping this is finally an opportunity to create their own state, and the Turks will be willing to do almost anything to stop that from happening, lest it reignite the recently quelled rebellion among their own Kurdish minority just across the border. (Turkey has already demanded that its army be the occupying force in northern Iraq as the price for letting the United States use its territory as a base during the war.) Some of the Shia in the south will try to turn their numerical dominance into political domination over the new Iraqi state being created under American tutelage, while others (quite possibly supported by Shia Iran) will scheme to create their own state in the south (which would totally panic their prospective neighbours in Kuwait and Saudi Arabia). The Sunni Arabs, deposed at last from their political domination of Iraq, will be embittered and could easily turn against the American occupation forces, especially if there was serious fighting and large loss of life among that community before Saddam's fall. And the United States "doesn't do nation-building."

Even if there have been no huge upheavals elsewhere in the region, this could be an extremely difficult and dangerous time in Iraq, and it's not clear that the Bush administration or the U.S. public is prepared for the cost in money and perhaps in American lives of a prolonged military occupation of Iraq. If the problem is compounded by other possible side effects of the war, such as an Islamist revolutionary government in Jordan or civil war in Saudi Arabia, it could become an extremely painful experience for Washington. If matters were to get sufficiently out of control in Iraq, it is imaginable that the Bush administration would simply pull American troops out (just as Clinton pulled American troops out of Somalia in 1993), leaving the country and the region mired in civil war and chaos. Bush is acutely aware that his father lost the 1992 presidential election only twenty months after winning the Gulf War in 1991, and will not wish a continuing flow of American casualties to blight his chances of re-election in 2004. But he might lose it anyway if the price of oil, which would almost certainly spike at $40 or $45 a barrel briefly when the war comes, should stay high for many months because of continuing turbulence and uncertainty in the region. This would cause a prolongation and deepening of the current recession in the U.S. and other industrialized countries.

Yet that could be the least bad outcome of the current adventure, if it discredited the pernicious doctrines of unilateralism and pre-emption that have recently taken root in Washington. For most of the past century, American idealism was the main driving force behind the effort to replace the old world of international anarchy, institutionalized injustice, and chronic war with a new system based on the rule of law. From the League of

Nations and the United Nations to the Nuremberg trials and the Universal Declaration of Human Rights, it was Americans who led the way, but now the temptations of sole superpower status and the ideological convictions of the neo-conservative élite are leading America in a different direction, one that is profoundly damaging to the world order previous generations of Americans worked so long to build.

The foundation on which all our new institutions have been built is the Treaty of Westphalia, which in 1648 ended a century of religious wars in Europe by recognizing the absolute sovereignty of every existing state. Westphalia deliberately subordinated freedom of conscience to the higher priority of domestic and international peace. *Cuius regio, eius religio* was the formula: if your king happens to be Protestant, then you have to be Protestant too, or else move. States were given absolute control over their own citizens, and guaranteed freedom from outside meddling, but there was no attempt to go beyond that and ban war entirely. The Treaty of Westphalia did not outlaw wars and forced border changes, because it was still dealing with a Europe of absolute monarchies. So long as religion was left out of it and popular passions were not aroused, limited wars for colonies and bits of border territory were manageable (and potentially quite profitable). Things only began to get out of hand with the advent of democracy.

This posed little problem for the earliest democratic revolutions, in the United States and France: you got rid of the king and just transferred your loyalty to "the people," who happened to share the same language and ethnicity anyway. But most of the world's existing states were empires, containing many different ethnic and linguistic groups, where democracy was dynamite. When democratic revolutions destroy the old hierarchies and loyalties, there is always an urgent need for some new focus of loyalty and identity, and the quick and dirty fix, in most cases, has been ethnicity. So the wars that broke up the empires and redefined borders in terms of ethnic nationalisms spread first across Europe, and then the rest of the world.

They were particularly savage wars, because the only kind of wars that democracies fight well are total wars. It is much easier to mobilize popular support for some allegedly high cause, where vital interests or even national survival is at stake, than for some more limited goal, so wars of nationalism are fought with no holds barred. By 1945, with the aid of modern science and technology, nationalist warmongers had produced both nuclear weapons and extermination camps.

The survivors of the Second World War were very frightened people: they had stared into the Pit, and it was filled with tens of millions of dead. So right after the war they created new global rules, ones that we all still live by. They were, of course, utterly contradictory.

To prevent new wars they created the United Nations, whose primary rule was that no country may ever change its borders by force, or even intervene in the internal affairs of another. The 1945 settlement in essence is "Westphalia plus." Under it, international war itself becomes illegal, except in defence of the borders as they existed at the time the UN Charter was signed, in which case collective military action to defend them becomes an international obligation. During the long Cold War between the West and the Soviet bloc that followed, the UN was widely regarded as a failed organization, but "Westphalia plus" really worked. Empires have been dismantled and federations have broken up, but not many international borders have been changed by force since 1945. Even the few enforced changes that did happen, like the Israeli conquest of the West Bank and Gaza Strip in 1967 or the Indonesian invasion of East Timor in 1975, have been treated as illegitimate and temporary by the UN and almost everybody else. And there has not, of course, been another world war.

The price of this settlement has been high. Absolute sovereignty means that every government can do whatever it likes to its own citizens with absolute impunity. It is a tyrants' charter, and from Cambodia in the years 1975–79 to Rwanda in 1994 it is ordinary people who have paid the price. Their only hope of assistance from outside – a pretty flimsy one, most of the time – has been the Universal Declaration of Human Rights. This document, passed by the UN in 1948 and ratified by almost every country in the world, addressed the other legacy of nationalist total war: the death camps. In direct but unacknowledged contradiction to the UN Charter, the declaration implies that the doctrine that the internal affairs of states were inviolate died with the Holocaust. Henceforward, the basic human rights enshrined in the Universal Declaration must be respected by all governments everywhere, regardless of ideology or circumstances.

The declaration was reinforced by the UN Convention on the Prevention and Punishment of the Crime of Genocide, also signed in 1948, but no enforcement mechanism was attached to it. Unless all the great powers on the Security Council could agree (which they very rarely could, given their mutual rivalries and fears), nothing much could be done by outsiders even about the most dreadful human rights abuses taking place within the borders of a sovereign state.

There were occasional and partial exceptions, like the international sanctions against apartheid South Africa, but by and large sovereignty trumped human rights until the 1990s. The most extreme case was Cambodia in the time of the Khmer Rouge: the UN took no notice as Pol Pot's regime carried out the worst genocide of the decade in 1975–79, but came to his defence when Cambodia's sovereignty was violated by Hanoi, which sent in the Vietnamese army in December 1978, ostensibly to save Cambodia's Vietnamese minority from extinction. The absolute primacy of sovereignty made sense in a world living under the shadow of global nuclear war, for nothing was worth risking that. But a world released from the imminent threat of nuclear holocaust by the end of the Cold War was bound to start paying more attention to human rights – especially because, in the meantime, changes in media technology had begun to bring the atrocities committed on the other side of the planet right into people's homes. "World public opinion" is no longer an empty phrase, and it does have a large moral dimension. Add the fact that the rapid spread of democracy after the mid-1980s gradually reduced the number of dictatorships to a minority of UN members no longer able to thwart any UN interventions in defence of human rights, and the new activism of the UN in the 1990s becomes perfectly understandable.

It was a highly tentative and nervous activism, for everybody was very aware that when you start playing around with doctrines of limited sovereignty, you are playing with fire. Nobody wanted to stand by and watch while a generation of Muslims was massacred in former Yugoslavia, and the guilt of having done exactly that in 1994 while a generation of Tutsis was massacred in Rwanda weighed heavily on the conscience of most leaders, but there was huge concern that in attacking Serbia and breaching the old absolute ban on intervening in a state's internal affairs the UN was setting a precedent that could easily be exploited by powerful states with more cynical agendas. In the end, the Security Council split the difference, more or less authorizing a "coalition of the willing" – in practice, the NATO countries – to take action on its behalf while stopping short of making it a full-fledged UN peace-enforcement operation. It worked, and the UN was sufficiently emboldened that when the United States went to the Security Council demanding authority to attack Afghanistan for harbouring the leaders of a terrorist organization and refusing to deliver them to justice, it was granted that authority without delay. A valuable body of precedent was being created, but it depended critically on states, and especially the most powerful states, not abusing the new rules by attacking other states that were not committing outright genocide or flagrantly sheltering major terrorist networks. Above all, they must not launch unilateral attacks without UN approval. But now the U.S. is challenging both the new rules and the old.

"The course of this nation does not depend on the decisions of others," declared Bush in his January 2003 State of the Union message. It was a declaration of independence from the world that drew prolonged applause from the joint houses of Congress. And he means it: in an earlier speech to West Point cadets in June 2002, he said, "The military must be ready to strike at a moment's notice in any dark corner of the world. All nations that decide for aggression and terror will pay a price." They will pay a price when the U.S. decides it is necessary, that is to say, without any obligation to refer to the international institutions we have spent generations to build, unless it's certain in advance they will agree to support the United States's position.

America has often ignored international institutions for pragmatic reasons, especially in an emergency, but to cement this into a doctrine is a long step farther into the past. That is what Richard Haass, director of policy planning at the State Department, was doing in April 2002 when he explained in a *New Yorker* interview: "Sovereignty entails obligations. One is not to massacre your own people. Another is not to support terrorism in any way. If a government fails to meet these obligations, then it forfeits some of the normal advantages of sovereignty, including the right to be left alone inside your own territory. Other governments, including the U.S., gain the right to intervene. In the case of terrorism this can even lead to a right of preventive, or peremptory, self-defense." Some of this is true enough, and unobjectionable, but Haass wasn't saying that the decision to pre-empt an anticipated attack must pass through the UN, or even command broad international support. He was asserting the right of the United States to attack other sovereign states unilaterally, without consultation or legal authority from the UN, whenever it feels threatened. Even if the United States ultimately extorts a form of consent to its attack on Iraq from a Security Council desperate to keep the U.S. from abandoning the UN system entirely, that would not soften the impact of Haass's assertion of America's right to act unilaterally in any significant way.

Generalize that rule and you have a world of nuclear-armed anarchy. The same argument would give India the right to attack Pakistan, even to launch a pre-emptive nuclear strike against Pakistan if it feels threatened – or vice versa, of course. It would give Israel the right to attack any Arab country that aspires to the same nuclear weapons that Israel already possesses in abundance – and any Arab country the right to hit Israel first if it suspects that such a strike is coming. Haass's declaration is American exceptionalism taken to the nth degree, but other states won't accept that this new doctrine applies only to the United States: what's sauce for the goose is sauce for the gander.

Yet it will be very hard to shift America from its present course, which was already set even before the terrorist attacks of September 11 reinforced the unilateralist trend.

Washington's post–Cold War triumphalism was already driving the Clinton administration to oppose any new international rules that might limit American freedom of action in the later 1990s, notably in the U.S. campaign against the treaty banning land mines and in American attempts to weaken the new International Criminal Court (including a law that dissenting congressmen ridiculed as the Netherlands Invasion Act, which authorized the U.S. government to use military force to free American citizens brought before the ICC in The Hague). Similarly, the cancellation of the Anti-Ballistic Missile Treaty, U.S. sabotage of new provisions for intrusive inspections under the Chemical Weapons Convention, and more recently Washington's rejection of similar attempts to write some provisions for enforcement into the Biological Weapons Treaty are not merely expressions of the neo-conservative philosophy that dominates the Bush administration. They are manifestations of a more generalized go-it-alone hubris among the Washington political and policy élite, most strikingly summarized by Andrew Bacevich, a retired U.S. army colonel and professor of international relations at Boston University, who wrote in a recent edition of the conservative foreign policy journal *The National Interest*: "In all of American public life, there is hardly a single prominent figure who finds fault with the notion of the United States remaining the world's sole military superpower until the end of time."

It is a preposterous ambition for a country with only 5 per cent of the world's people, and a population that has absolutely no appetite for high casualties or high taxes. It is bound to be abandoned sooner or later, after more or less painful experiences turn the American public against it. Sooner would be better, but one would not wish that it comes about at the expense of a calamity in the Middle East. Nevertheless, that may well be the ultimate result of the war against Iraq and the subsequent occupation – a silver lining of the most tarnished sort to what is otherwise likely to be a fairly grim episode.

The other area where the American attack on Iraq could do great damage is in retarding or distorting the spread of democracy to the Arab world, currently the world's most deprived region in that regard. This is despite the fact that the United States has recently changed its tune, at least in declared policy, and now officially favours democracy in the Arab countries. Secretary of State Colin Powell did a public U-turn in December 2002, acknowledging in a speech to the Heritage Foundation in Washington that "Too many Middle Easterners are ruled by closed political systems" and stating that "We believe that democracy and free markets will benefit all countries in the Middle East." If it were seriously meant, this shift in policy should have caused flat panic in American client regimes like those of Saudi Arabia, Egypt, and Algeria, but there was little sign of panic in the relevant quarters – perhaps because Richard Haass, in another speech a few days previously, had promised that "the U.S. will support the democratic process, even if it produces policies not to our liking" – but then hedged his bets by warning that "unrestrained zeal" for democratic change on the part of the United States could "make matters worse rather than better."

To put it more plainly, if there were genuinely free elections throughout the Arab world later this year, they would produce an unbroken sweep of anti-American governments from Morocco to Yemen. This is not because Arabs support the terrorists who "hate our freedoms," as Bush likes to put it. The terrorists couldn't care less about America's freedoms, and the broad majority of Arabs actually admire and envy them. What they hate is America's policies in the Middle East: its reflex support for Israel, and its perennial support for corrupt, oppressive Arab regimes that do America's bidding. If that were to change, America would once again be the anti-imperialist beacon of democracy that it seemed to be to so many Arabs in the 1950s, but in the short run, at least, it is most unlikely to change. At least, the people on the ground don't believe it is going to change.

That is why a recent survey of public opinion by the Washington-based Pew Research Center in two key Arab countries, Egypt and Jordan, and two important non-Arab Muslim countries in the region, Turkey and Pakistan, found unfavourable opinions of the United States, based on the assumption that the war against Iraq is an attempt to impose a new American settlement in the region that ensures access to oil and security for Israel, that ranged from 60 to 70 per cent in the first three countries and reached 90 per cent in Pakistan. A classified opinion survey carried out by the Saudi Arabian interior ministry in October 2002 found that 95 per cent of educated Saudis in the 28–41 age group agreed with Osama bin Laden's views on America. All of these countries' governments are America's allies in the war on terror, which suggests that they are skating on thin ice. And most of the people longing and even fighting for democracy throughout the region would say that the current American policy is likely to damage the prospects for democracy in the Arab world, not enhance them. Are they right? That depends on whether there is some specific problem in Arab or Muslim culture that impedes the shift to democracy, or whether the Arabs have just been unlucky so far. It would help if we understood how democratic revolutions have evolved.

The dominant political trend of the past two centuries, infecting first the West and then spreading to the rest of the planet, has been democracy. It is virtually irresistible because it is driven by the interaction between human nature and the technology of mass communications, rather than by some specific set of cultural beliefs. Before mass communications, mass societies could not be democratic: it was technically impossible. But by the same token, it turns out, any country where the millions *can* talk to one another through mass media is heading for democracy within a couple of generations. Not free, uncensored mass media, let alone good, responsible mass media – just mass media.

And not just Western countries, either. There is a myth, much cherished in the United States in particular, that democracy is a gift from Christian Westerners who were fortunate enough to have classical Greeks up their family tree (and particularly from the English-speaking peoples) to the lesser breeds without the law. This is based on the assumption that democracy is a philosophical breakthrough of the eighteenth-century European Enlightenment, not an innate value shared by all human beings and equally accessible by all cultures. Yet the founding fathers of the American Revolution and the *philosophes* who laid the groundwork for the French Revolution would not have agreed: they believed that democratic revolutions would allow all human beings to regain that equality that everybody's ancestors had enjoyed before the creation of the mass civilizations, back in the time of what Jean-Jacques Rousseau called the "Noble Savage" – hunter-gatherers, to use the more modern term. Even the word "revolution," in its original sense, meant a turning back to an idealized past – and it turns out that the original meaning was probably correct.

While Rousseau's romanticism about hunter-gatherers was overdone – there is a great deal of violence in and between such groups – he has been proved right by modern anthropology in his key assumptions that they lived as equals, shared resources, made decisions by discussion and consensus, and had no autocratic leaders. This is only true of genuine hunter-gatherers who live in very small societies, typically in bands of less than one hundred and fifty people, but that describes the totality of the human race for 95 per cent of its history on this planet. The values of egalitarian hunter-gatherer societies are default-mode human values, and remained almost universal among human beings until the advent of large-scale societies some thousands of years ago – at which point they vanished almost completely from the historical record. All mass societies from Sumeria down to the eighteenth century were militarized tyrannies based on a hierarchy of privilege. In larger societies, equality before the law and democratic decision-making were completely absent, probably because they had become technically impossible. The problem of numbers would not permit it.

Once an early human society grew beyond a few thousand members, decision-making by the old consensus-based model became impossible, and egalitarian values had to give way to centralized authority if this more complex society was to function at all. Inevitably, there were willing volunteers for the role of chief, and the chiefs grew into god-kings as the societies grew into the millions. So it continued for many thousands of years, and one would think that the old values had been utterly forgotten if it were not for occasional city-states where democracy was practised by a privileged, numerically small minority, and for the intriguing emergence of new universal religions like Buddhism, Christianity, and Islam that preached human equality in this endless wasteland of autocracy. As recently as five hundred years ago, there was absolutely no evidence to suggest that Christian European societies had more democratic potential than Muslim Arab ones. Then suddenly, in the latter half of the second millennium AD, mass democracies started struggling to be born in the West, and so people have traditionally assumed that it must have had something to do with Western culture, but the evidence of recent events suggests that there may be a simpler, mostly technological explanation. The earliest mass democracies occurred in the places where there was already the beginning of what we now call mass communications – just the printing press and widespread literacy for the first century or so, but even that was enough to create the possibility of an egalitarian mass society that based its decisions on discussion and consensus. For the first time since mass societies emerged, it was possible for their members to hear one another, and to have a kind of conversation about the issues that mattered to them.

In other words, it became possible to turn back to the ancient human values, and to recreate in a modified form the society of equals that was once the normal way of life for everybody – and wherever the possibility arose, people tried to seize it. Overthrowing the old regimes was a bloody business in many cases, and devising mechanisms for running these new societies of equals fairly and efficiently is a task that is still not complete more than two centuries later, but by the end of the eighteenth century there were several democratic societies numbering in the millions, and by the end of the nineteenth century there were several dozen. All in the West, of course, which led to many illusions about the specific cultural roots of democracy in the West, but the more relevant fact was that there were almost no non-Western mass societies with access to mass media in their own language until well into the twentieth century. Now we know for certain that democracy is not a Western phenomenon: if China had been the first country to perfect printing and achieve mass literacy, then the Chinese would probably have had the first successful democratic revolution in a mass society.

The twentieth century was largely taken up with dealing with various perversions of democracy like fascism and communism, which decreed equality for only one ethnic group or class, and as late as the 1970s there were few democratic non-Western societies except those that had inherited the system from their former colonial rulers and managed to hang on to at least the forms of it. But a new style of non-violent revolution was already being sketched out in countries like Iran, and in the later 1980s it suddenly took off.

Non-violent political protest has a long pedigree in the twentieth century, and its two most distinguished proponents, Mohandas Gandhi and Martin Luther King, enjoy the status of secular saints. But both Gandhi and King were struggling against essentially democratic and law-bound governments: until the 1970s, all discussions of non-violence's potential for effecting real political change tended to end with the observation that it wouldn't have worked against Hitler or Stalin. But then, in 1986, the Filipinos successfully used it against a dictator. The Philippines was a good place to start, because it was a media-wise country whose opposition leaders were well aware of both the Asian and the American traditions of non-violence. Moreover, the People Power revolution in Manila was the first popular uprising where there was television coverage with live satellite uplinks, and its leaders brilliantly exploited their direct access to a global audience to deter

President Ferdinand Marcos from a violent response. But if a dictatorship loses its will to use force, it is finished: get on the helicopter quick, and to hell with Imelda's shoes.

The methodology used in the Manila revolution was broadcast around the world, and other Asians were quick to pick it up. In the next three years there were successful copycat non-violent revolutions against dictators in Bangladesh, Thailand, and South Korea (plus a tragic failure in Burma in 1988, where media coverage was sparse and the generals were not deterred from slaughtering thousands of protestors in the streets). Then, in May-June 1989, students in the People's Republic of China tried the same tactics. They failed in the end, but for three weeks they hovered on the brink of some sort of success while the whole world watched. Subsequently, I interviewed a number of the students who led the Tiananmen Square occupation, and most confirmed that in 1988 and early 1989 they were conducting what amounted to clandestine seminars in non-violence at Beijing University. They were deliberately studying Gandhi, King, and videotapes of the events in Manila and elsewhere with the idea that the same tactics might work even in China. Then they road-tested them.

We will not know how close they came to success until the archives of the Chinese Communist Party are opened, years or even decades from now. But the late 1980s showed that this was a one-size-fits-all technique, equally available to people of any culture. More importantly, it showed that people belonging to almost every major culture in the world – Christian Filipinos, Buddhist Thais, Muslim Bangladeshis, Confucian Chinese –

were as eager to overthrow their autocrats as Europeans had been in the past. In fact, it was the Chinese who showed the Eastern Europeans how to do it using the new techniques, for the whole world saw these tactics apparently coming close to success in a *Communist* capital – including, most importantly, the East Germans, a majority of whom lived in easy reach of West German television signals. Less than six months later, having taken note of their own regime's isolation, the East Germans took to the streets of Leipzig and Berlin and used the same tactics with total success. They correctly calculated that the local Communists, unlike the Chinese variety, had lost the will to massacre their own citizens – and once that was clear, the game was quickly over, not only in East Germany but all over the Soviet bloc. Three hundred and seventy-five million people in what are now two dozen countries removed their rulers and dismantled an empire with hardly a shot fired.

There have been quite a few shots fired subsequently, mostly in the mountainous and ethnically tangled southern border-lands of the former Soviet empire. Those borderlands con-tained many Muslim subject peoples, and while most got freedom, some, like the Chechnyans and the Bosnians, got war with their more numerous Christian neighbours. But that is just the usual post-imperial turmoil. The revolution itself was bloodless almost everywhere, and despite the economic mis-eries that the transition has brought to many people, the planet is a much better and safer place as a result. No more gulags, no more obsessive discussions of nuclear throw-weight, no more bipolar world where to reject the local orthodoxy was to defect. It was the first time that Asia has led the way politically for at least several hundred years, and the scope for non-violent action in a media-saturated world has continued to show its power in the years since in new democratic revolutions from South Africa to Indonesia. In fifteen years we have gone from a world where two-thirds of the people lived under tyrannies to a world where more than two-thirds of the people live in more or less democratic societies, and we have done so without the great explosions of violence that historically accompanied change on this scale.

So why have all these developments passed the Arab world by? Are they likely to happen there any time soon? And will the attack on Iraq and its likely repercussions around the Arab world facilitate the spread of democracy (as the United States claims), or slow it down and divert it?

Much of the rage and violence that disfigures the Arab world is connected with this democratic deficit: frustrated and powerless people can be walking timebombs. And it is a problem specific to the 300 million people of the Arab world, not to the broader world of Islam: more than half of the billion Muslims who are not Arabs, from Turkey to Indonesia, live in functioning democracies. Part of the reason for the Arab world's political backwardness is certainly the curse of oil, which has led foreigners to meddle non-stop in the Middle East, and the half-century of confrontation with Israel, marked by repeated Arab defeats, has also played a role. But the situation is probably about to change, because at last there is uncensored news available in Arabic.

The Arab world never had uncensored news and free debate until five years ago, when al-Jazeera went on the air. It's only a single television channel, but it broadcasts by satellite twenty-four hours a day, and can be picked up by anybody with a dish almost anywhere in the Arab world.

Al-Jazeera has six hundred journalists operating in all the Arab capitals (except those where they have been expelled), plus London, Paris, New York, and Washington, and it has single-handedly transformed the nature of political debate everywhere in the Arab world. It has interviewed Israeli cabinet ministers live. It has broadcast tapes sent to it by Osama bin Laden. It has allowed Saudi Arabian dissidents to criticize the monarchy. It has even given air time to critics of the Qatar government where it is based.

This may seem like no big thing. After all, it's only one channel, and you have to be rich enough to own a dish to get it. But that is to misunderstand the nature of the media environment. When a major outlet starts to tell the truth, even if only one Arab in ten sees it (al-Jazeera claims a regular audience of 35 million), the word gets around very fast.

Al-Jazeera grew out a failed attempt by the British Broadcasting Corporation to create an Arabic-language TV service. It was a joint venture with a Saudi company that tried to censor a documentary hostile to the Saudi regime, so the BBC pulled out – leaving behind a talented team of Arab TV journalists who had got a whiff of editorial freedom. They went to Sheikh Hamad bin Khalifa al-Thani, the British-educated ruler of the small Gulf state of Qatar, and pitched the idea of al-Jazeera to him.

They picked the right man. Only recently come to power, he was starting to introduce democracy in his own tiny sheikhdom, and was so attracted by the idea of providing uncensored news to the whole Arab world that he agreed to bankroll the channel to the tune of $150 million over five years. It still isn't making a profit – partly because a lot of local companies, and some multinational ones too, have been instructed not to advertise on al-Jazeera – but in five years it has transformed the political environment in the Middle East.

Even bad, censored, lying media can be the godmother to a democratic revolution, because people become very adept at reading between the lines and seem to understand instinctively that the mere existence of mass media means that we can now run our own affairs. But good media that don't lie can accelerate the process a great deal.

The free flow of information opens people's minds, and then change can happen. "I think that if al-Jazeera had been there fifteen years ago, there would have been no September 11," said al-Jazeera's marketing director, Ali Mohammad Kamal, in October 2002. If it is still in business fifteen years from now, there will be a lot fewer dictatorships and absolute monarchies in the Arab world. And if it is not, then many other satellite channels will take its place, together with a hundred thousand Web sites, Arabic-language newspapers printed abroad, and uncensored Arabic-language radio services broadcasting into the Arab world. One way or another, the jig is up for the traditional authoritarian Arab regimes, though it may take some time and a great deal of upheaval to work through the turbulence associated with the change.

Could the U.S. attack on Iraq derail this process? Not entirely, but the backlash to a major U.S. military intervention in the Arab world could divert the flow of change into so-called "Islamic democracies," which are not what anybody really needs at this point. Iran has spent twenty-five years stuck in that detour, and is still waiting for the real democracy that most people were seeking in the 1978 revolution. No doubt the Iranians will finish the job one of these days, but a whole generation has been wasted. The Arabs have waited long enough already.

Readers of this book will know a lot more about outcomes when they pick it up than I do as I finish it on February 10, 2003, but two predictions seem safe. At least the end of the Cold War and the dismantling of the global alliance systems mean that war in the Middle East no longer brings with it the possibility of a superpower confrontation and a worldwide nuclear war, as it did several times in the past. The Third World War has been cancelled, and however bad it gets in the Middle East, that is where the fighting stays. And al-Qaeda and its sister organizations will still be around when the fighting is over, perhaps only a little bit strengthened, perhaps a great deal. As Stella Rimington, former head of Britain's Security Service (MI5), said in the *Guardian* in September 2002: "Terrorism did not begin on September 11 and it will not end there. . . . The history of terrorism in the twentieth century shows that a 'war on terrorism' cannot be won, unless the causes of terrorism are eradicated by making the world a place free of grievances, something that will not happen. Terrorism has proved so effective in catching the world's attention and even, ultimately, in achieving the terrorists' objectives, that it will continue to appeal to extremists. However good our counter measures, some of it will succeed, but it can be made more difficult."

That is not being done. Even if things go relatively well in the attack on Iraq, it is fair to observe that U.S. Secretary of Defense Donald Rumsfeld is moonlighting as the director of recruitment for al-Qaeda. If things go badly, he may be instrumental in helping that organization to achieve its ultimate goal: bringing Islamist extremists to power in some major Arab state. That is not what he intends, of course, but it could still happen.

If we could sneak a look at Rumsfeld's agenda for March, it would probably go a bit like this:

17 March: Attack Iraq. Special Forces to seize oil fields. Drop off dry cleaning.

20 March: 10th Mountain Division enters Baghdad. NSC meeting p.m. Condi's b/day: flowers?

22 March: Victory press conf. @ Pentagon. Regrets re Saddam shot while trying to escape. Collect dry cleaning on way home.

It could happen exactly like that too – if all the U.S. technology works perfectly, and nobody in Iraq fights back, and everybody else in the Middle East behaves. But there is another possible timetable, which goes like this:

17 March: U.S. attacks Iraq. Saddam blows oil fields. Anti-American riots in Jordan, Egypt, and Pakistan. Iraq fires Scud missiles at Israel.

18 March: Israel fires a hundred missiles at Iraq. Riots intensify throughout Muslim world. Hezbollah launches a hundred Katyushas into northern Israel from southern Lebanon.

19 March: Israel invades southern Lebanon. Coup in Pakistan; new government orders U.S. forces out. Islamist Palestinians overthrow king of Jordan and cancel peace treaty with Israel.

20 March: 10th Mountain Division enters suburbs of Baghdad; severe street-fighting. Israeli forces start to push Palestinians out of West Bank into Jordan; fighting at Allenby Bridge.

21 March: Saudi Arabian National Guard rebels; civil war in Arabia. New Pakistan government declares it will make nuclear weapons available to Arab states confronting Israel. U.S. casualties in Battle of Baghdad pass two hundred; first use of chemical weapons; spot oil price reaches $85 a barrel.

22 March: Rumsfeld resigns; forgets to pick up dry cleaning.

I don't know which way Rumsfeld's War will come out; I cannot read the future. But if even a third of the pessimistic projections were to come true, it would make this the most counterproductive war since Napoleon's invasion of Russia. It would not have hurt to give the UN arms inspectors a little more time.

When you start a "pre-emptive" war, you are in effect deciding that all these people must die right now to avoid something bad happening in the future. It is almost impossible to make that equation work for the attack on Iraq, because with UN arms inspectors all over the country it was certainly not the time Saddam Hussein would choose to hand over some of his chemical or biological weapons (if he had any) to his terrorist friends (if he had any). Waiting six months or even a year for the UN inspectors to find the weapons of mass destruction, or to confirm that they're not there, would have been a good deal saner and more humane than plunging into the unknown. Even if the war causes none of the larger disasters that are possible, it still involves too many deaths for too little gain.

ACKNOWLEDGEMENTS

I wrote this book in three and a half weeks, on the road half the time (and only half awake some of the time). So I owe a special thanks to my editor, Dinah Forbes, my copy editor, Heather Sangster, my wife, Tina Viljoen, and my two sons, Evan Dyer and Owen Dyer, both trained historians and now experienced journalists, for working on the manuscript and saving me from a hundred errors and omissions. Thanks also to my old friend Heino Kopietz, who has forgotten more about the Arab world than I will ever know.

Any remaining errors and omissions are entirely their fault, of course. I was probably asleep at the time.